RAKSHA BANDHAN

JANMASHTAMI

GANESH CHATURTHI

HARVEST

ROSH HASHANNAH

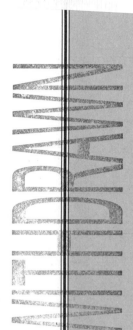

DIWALI

GURU PURB –
GURU NANAK'S BIRTHDAY

HANUKKAH

CHRISTMAS

INTRODUCTION

Religious festivals are one of the ways in which people of a faith celebrate their unity – their belonging together. They are a means of remembering who we are and where we belong, of linking past roots to the here and now and to hope for the future. Festivals are very much part of the life of almost every primary school and increasingly teachers are focusing on the religious festivals celebrated by their pupils.

Essentially festivals are an outward expression of the symbolic inner meanings and beliefs of commitment and, although much may be transmitted through stories, activities and rituals, it is important that we do not just give children these aspects without some exploration of the symbolic and inner meanings a festival has for the particular celebrating faith community.

We can think of any festival as having a number of essential elements, each of which has significance in the celebration. Maurice Lynch, Director of the BFSS National RE Centre at the West London Institute, identifies five such elements: rituals, symbols, community (past, present and future), stories and inner meanings.

As teachers, care and sensitivity are vital when looking at religious festivals and it is important to remember that not all festivals are equally significant in all faiths and that not all members of any religion celebrate a festival in the same way. A Muslim festival such as Eid-Ul-Fitr may have different traditions associated with it according to the country or particular community; and many Hindu festivals are celebrated in India in different ways depending on the region of the country; indeed some are peculiar to a particular state or part of the country. Equally, members of a religion such as Hinduism who have settled abroad may have adapted their ways of celebrating. So we must beware of saying, or implying that, for example, all Hindus celebrate Diwali in such and such a way. It is far better to say 'these are some of the ways Hindus like to celebrate Diwali' or 'this is how many Hindus celebrate'.

In this book are some of the festivals celebrated by the six major world faiths: Buddhism, Christianity, Hinduism, Islam, Judaism and Sikhism. The festivals are arranged in calendar order from January through to December. Ramadan/Eid-Ul-Fitr has been placed according to the time it occurred when this book was compiled but its occurrence is determined by the lunar calendar and so it may fall at any time during the year. Other festivals such as Easter, Passover and Diwali do not fall on a particular date in the Gregorian Calendar.

Some teachers may wish to look at a group of festivals together; thus Wesak, Janmashtami, Ganesh Chaturthi, Guru Purb and Christmas might be explored as birth festivals, or Diwali, Guru Purb, Hanukkah and Christmas could be looked at as festivals of light.

Each section has a short introduction about the festival and contains stories, poems and songs. The book includes material which children across the whole primary age range should enjoy and the Key Stages 1 and 2 poems, songs and stories index on pages 190–191 gives an indication of whether a particular item is appropriate for KS1, KS2 or both.

(A note about spelling: for several of the festivals there are a number of alternative spellings which are accepted Romanised approximations of the name in the original language; where alternatives have been used by the authors these have not been standardised.)

Jill Bennett

CHINESE NEW YEAR

Chinese New Year, the Spring Festival, falls on a different date each year (usually between mid-January and mid-February) because the Chinese follow a lunar calendar and it marks the beginning of the Chinese Lunar Year. It is the most important Chinese festival of the year and is celebrated by Chinese communities and families all over the world. The festivities last for 15 days culminating in the Festival of Lanterns. Although the origins of the festival are religious, and there are rituals honouring domestic gods, the major part of the celebrations are secular.

Traditionally this is the time for new beginnings, for settling debts, for completing any home repairs, for spring cleaning and for honouring ancestors.

On New Year's Eve special foods such as dumplings, cakes and biscuits are baked; homes are decorated with spring flowers and fruits; and red banners of silk, satin or paper bearing New Year greetings of the motto 'Longevity, prosperity, happiness and harmony', written in gold, are hung up. New Year's Eve dinner is a family gathering when special efforts are made to get together. The New Year is welcomed at midnight with firecrackers and incense. These are to welcome back the kitchen god who returns from a visit to the Emperor of Heaven where a report has been made on each family.

Early the following morning, New Year's Day, everyone washes and puts on new or best clothes, traditionally red, pink, orange or yellow, ready to go visiting relations and friends. A traditional breakfast including New Year's cake – rice flour steamed in sugar – is eaten. Children wish their parents a Happy New Year 'Kung Hey Fat Choy' and in return may receive sweets or preserved fruits – symbols of sweet harmony – and little red packets called Lai See or lucky money envelopes. The front door is kept open to allow visitors to enter without knocking, although some may announce their arrival by dropping Lai See through the letter box.

For Chinese people New Year in particular is a time for acknowledging family loyalties and for showing respect to elders.

Yuan Tan – Chinese New Year

Time now
when days are turning
from the greys of winter to
the coming spring
time now
for burning of
the kitchen gods.
Their smoke, unfurled,
will take our message
to the gods on high.

Time now for dancing.
For the Lion who will bring
good fortune. Banish
evil from the world.
Time for gifts. To light
the fireworks of hope.
To try. Look forward.
Have no fear.
This is New Year.

Ann Bonner

The monster and the villagers

Long, long ago in China, in the villages around Shanghai, all the villagers lived in terror because of a huge monster who prowled in the nearby hills. Every evening as darkness fell he would come down to one of the villages, destroy crops and capture one of the villagers to eat for his supper. The villagers were much too frightened to try and fight the monster. They just did not know what to do: for three hundred and sixty five days a year they lived in fear of their lives.

Then late one afternoon a young girl was just collecting the clothes she had washed earlier in the day when she saw the monster coming towards her. The poor girl could not run away and was much too panic stricken even to scream. On the tree beside her was a length of red cloth which she'd hung from the branches to dry. Closer and closer came the monster. All of a sudden a gust of wind caught the red cloth and it began to flap up and down. The monster let out a wild howl, turned tail and fled in the direction of the hills.

That monster never appeared again. Now at the time of New Year people remember the monster and hang red banners on their doors to ward off evil.

Colin J. Bennett

John and the green dragon

John lay in bed asleep. He was dreaming of cars, motorbikes and flying into danger with Batman.

Downstairs his mother, father and two big brothers were busy in the family restaurant. The Hong Kong Chinese Restaurant stood in a row of shops in the high street of a small, country town. The neon light flashed on and off all day and night 'TAKE AWAY...TAKE AWAY...'. People did indeed come to take away a delicious, hot bag of Chinese food and rush home to eat it in front of the television. Other people liked to have a meal out just for a treat, and they would come into the restaurant and sit under the red-tasselled lanterns, leaning over the menu with watering mouths.

It was the night of the Chinese New Year. The swing doors flapped to and fro as steaming dishes were carried through to hungry people. Chicken with sliced almonds, green peppers and special fried rice at Table 26; shark fin soup followed by crispy duck and bamboo shoots at Table 11; spare ribs in black bean sauce, sweet and sour pork, bird's nest soup and beef chop suey all at Table 5....the smells wafted upstairs, but John did not stir. Not so long ago he had had his favourite supper of egg, sausages, baked beans and chips.

Outside, the moon hung like a great lantern. Suddenly a shadow darkened the moonlit sky. John awoke. He could hear a rustling and whirling – like wind; a crackling and sparkling – like a fire; a looping and swooping – like waves. Outside his window John saw a green head bobbing up and down – a dragon's head – with red, glowing eyes and a long, flaming tongue darting in and out between huge, spiky, white teeth. The dragon squeezed himself between the open windows. His jagged, green body and long, long tail came trailing inside and coiled itself around the room like a giant kite.

'Hello,' said John politely. 'Can I help you?'

'I've flown all the way from China,' said the Green Dragon. 'Over snowy mountains and icy lakes; winding rivers and smoking factories; over vast fields of rice and wheat – and now I am so hungry I could swallow up your mother's kitchen.'

'Oh please don't do that,' cried John. 'My mother and father are very proud of their kitchen. They say that we cook the best Chinese food outside London. I help too with sorting out the knives, forks and spoons, and our customers call me Hong Kong John.'

Well then, Hong Kong John,' said the Green Dragon, 'since I am so hungry, and since it is the Chinese New Year, I think I should savour some of your famous food. After all – I am an expert. I have eaten at the finest tables in China – at feasts given by the great emperors themselves!'

'You must be very old if you have eaten with the emperors of China,' said John.

'Several hundred – maybe even a thousand,' boasted the dragon. 'Now then – about this food – I would like to eat deep fried pork with delectable seaweed; braised beef with soya sauce and noodles; bean curd with crab meat; king fried prawns with heavenly vegetables of the four seasons; but to start with I must sharpen my teeth on succulent spare ribs, and I'll finish with a bowl of lychees to sweeten me up. All this must be accompanied with a constant flow of hot, sweet-scented jasmine tea – pots and pots of it. Well? What are you waiting for?' The Green Dragon looked at John impatiently.

'I....I can't get all *that*!' gasped John.

'Can't you?' The dragon looked downcast. He whisked his tail and ground his teeth. 'Well, what can you get me then?' he asked sulkily.

'I might be able to get you something from the set menus,' said John. 'You know – select a dish from A, B, C or D – and you get three courses all for 80p.'

The Green Dragon heaved and rumbled. 'I don't care what you get me, anything, but get it fast before I start nibbling your curtains. I am absolutely starving!'

John crept downstairs. He peered through the bamboo screens at the bustling restaurant. His brothers looked like jugglers as they balanced plates and dishes piled high as pagodas, hurrying with orders from table to table. His father was mixing drinks at the bar, while his mother bent over sizzling saucepans in the kitchen behind. John tiptoed to the corner of the kitchen where they prepared the set menus. Taking one or two silver foil boxes he quickly scooped in some fried rice, chicken chop suey, a pancake roll, few crispy balls of sweet and sour pork and a pineapple fritter. The dragon sucked everything into his mouth – boxes and all! 'Where is the tea...I must have some tea – I did tell you....'

'I really could not manage tea,' said John, hoping that the dragon was not going to make trouble. 'I can get lemonade.' After gulping down several bottles of lemonade, the dragon licked his lips, stretched till it seemed he would push through the ceiling, then pointed his head towards the window. 'Are you ready to go?'

'Ready to go?' asked John, puzzled. 'Go where?'

'Why, to London of course,' said the dragon. 'I've come thousands of miles to see the New Year celebrations in.... What is the name of that place... So... Ho...?'

'Soho!' cried John – 'but that's a hundred miles from here.'

'I came from China in only a moment or two, we'll be in London in a jiffy,' boasted the dragon. Filled with excitement, John clambered on to the dragon's back and snuggled between his great wings with his arms clasped around his neck. 'Which way?' asked the dragon as they rose high into the sky.

'We always go up the motorway,' replied John.

The motorway shone below them in the moonlight like a winding silver ribbon. The cars and lorries flitted to and fro like dazzling insects. The next moment London lay below them – a million scattered lights. They swooped down over the river Thames and followed it up to

Westminster. They turned left at Big Ben, up Pall Mall, past the Horse Guards, over Trafalgar Square and up to Piccadilly. Suddenly a rocket sped up into the air showering them with sparks. 'I think we've arrived,' said the Green Dragon.

John could see a flutter of red flags and fairy lights garlanded across the street from roof-top to roof-top. Clashing cymbals and rattling drums filled the air. Laughing people danced about wearing strange masks, carrying streamers and gaily painted lanterns. A great paper lion wheeled in and out of the crowd, roaring and leaping as children chased and teased it.

'They must have known I was coming!' yelled the dragon. 'Look! They've hung the cabbages from their windows for me – I love cabbages.'

From almost every window, John could see Chinese cabbages dangling from the ends of string. For a moment the noise and frenzy of the crowd hushed in amazement as the Green Dragon came rushing in among them. Then there was a cheer of joy and everyone burst out laughing and shouting as the dragon zig-zagged from window to window gobbling up the cabbages. Children followed, pressing red-dyed melon seeds into John's hands and tossing red envelopes up to him with gifts inside. All around fireworks sprayed the sky and firecrackers spluttered at their feet.

'It's years since I saw a dragon dance,' murmured an elderly Chinese shopkeeper.

As the dance grew wilder, John's arms began to ache. He felt as if he were on a merry-go-round which would not stop. At last he could hold on no longer; his tired fingers loosened and he began to slide off the dragon's back. The dragon rollicked on through the crowd. John slithered to the ground, and before he could look around he was swept away by merry-makers and dancers. He tried to struggle after the Green Dragon, but gradually he found himself carried out of sight – down the side streets and up narrow alleys. Just as he was beginning to feel very lost, he felt a hand in his and turned to find a little girl at his side.

'You are the dragon boy, aren't you?' she said.

'Yes, but I've lost him,' said John sadly, 'and I can't get home without him.'

'Oh, don't worry,' replied the little girl, 'he'll find you when it's time. What is your name?'

'John,' said John, 'but some people call me Hong Kong John. My Chinese name is Ying-Chai.'

'Ying-Chai!' the little girl exclaimed. 'I like that for it means "Very Brave" and you must be brave to ride on a dragon's back. My name is Hoi-Au which means "Seagull". My English name is Marina.'

The children gaily jostled along the streets, chewing on melon seeds and dodging the firecrackers.

'I feel as if I were in China,' shouted John.

'Well, people do call this place "China Town" as there are many Chinese families living round here. Come and visit my house, we are nearly there.' They stopped outside a curio shop filled with Chinese statuettes of jade and marble; paintings and ornaments; precious silks and manuscripts.

'This is my father's shop,' said Marina. 'We live upstairs above the shop.'

John followed Marina upstairs and entered a room full of friendly people. They all turned with smiling faces and outstretched hands of welcome to greet them. Marina's mother came forward. 'Hello, dragon boy, I am delighted to have you in my home.' She bowed, then put a hand on his shoulder and gently sat him down as she could see that he was tired.

'His name is Ying-Chai,' Marina told them. Then everyone gathered round him and offered him Chinese sweets – salted, dried apricots, sweet and sour bananas; and there were bowls of prawn crackers and hot tea and lemonade.

John met the rest of Marina's family.

'These are my two brothers and sister. We are all at school in the neighbourhood. This is my most respected eldest uncle, Mr Tsin. He owns a restaurant just round the corner. My most honoured grandfather is Mr Leung and he owns a book shop two streets away.' John bowed deeply to Mr Tsin and Mr Leung, and they bowed back to him.

'My family have a restaurant miles out of London in the country,' John contributed.

Everyone smiled. The night passed. A sudden swell of sound from the crowd sent everyone running to the window. John saw the Green Dragon being carried along by cheering merry-makers. As they drew near, the dragon called up to the window where John was leaning out anxiously, 'It's time to go home now, John!'

John turned to Marina and her family and wished them good-bye. 'Thank you for looking after me,' he said, 'and I hope you will visit me in the country, one day.'

The dragon hovered outside the window and John climbed out on to his back.

'Good-bye, John! Good-bye, Ying-Chai, brave dragon boy!' called his friends.

As the dragon turned westwards, the first glow of dawn was beginning to light up the horizon behind them. The last rocket spluttered to the ground, and the lanterns already looked dimmer by the new light of day. John saw no more. The dragon flew back down the motorway with the boy fast asleep between his wings. A few early morning workers, who happened to glance up at the sky, were amazed to see such a high-flying kite with its long, long tail trailing among the pink-streaked clouds.

The next morning John awoke to find his mother by his bed. 'Happy New Year, John,' she beamed. 'Welcome to the Year of the Dragon. Here is a parcel which has come all the way from your uncle in China.'

John carefully unwrapped the paper and uncovered a large, flat box. Hardly daring to breathe, he lifted the lid. There lay a huge, green, paper kite shaped like a dragon, with red, glowing eyes, a long, flaming tongue between spiky white teeth.

'I've flown all the way from China...,' the dragon seemed to be saying, '...over snowy mountains and icy lakes; winding rivers and smoking factories... vast fields of rice and wheat... and ....'

Jamila Gavin

Chinese New Year

Low Siew Poh

Merrily

1. Chi-nese New Year is here a-gain, Here a-gain, here a-gain,

Chi-nese New Year is here a-gain, Let us now re-joice.

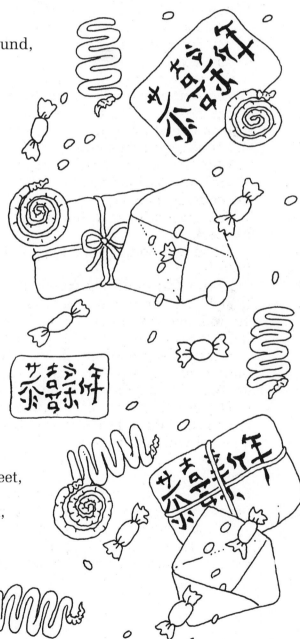

2. Down in the streets the crackers sound,
Crackers sound, crackers sound,
Down in the streets crackers sound,
Bing, bing, bang bang bong.

3. Children darting here and there,
Here and there, here and there,
Children darting here and there
Hee, hee, ha, ha, ha.

4. Look over there I see a lion,
See a lion, see a lion,
Look over there I see a lion,
Prancing up and down.

5. In every house the elders shout,
Elders shout, elders shout,
In every house the elders shout,
Yam Seng.

6. Children all get red packets,
Red packets, red packets,
Children all get red packets,
From everyone.

7. When friends meet they all will greet,
All will greet, all will greet,
When friends meet they all will greet,
Kong Hee Fatt Choy.

8. Let us then all celebrate,
Celebrate, celebrate,
Let us all then celebrate,
Happy New Year.

Chinese New Year

Dirt and dust is swept and gone,
Only Good Luck from now on.
Mother lays out fruits and sweets,
Entertainment in the streets.
Clash of cymbals,
Bang of drums,
'Make way!
Make way!
The lion comes.'
Brave and fearless,
Red and gold.
Welcome New Year,
Good-bye Old.

Ian Larmont

Chinese New Year dragon

There's a brightly coloured dragon swaying down the street,
Stomping and stamping and kicking up its feet.

There's a multi-coloured dragon – green and gold and red –
Twisting and twirling and shaking its head.

There's a silky-scaled dragon parading through the town,
Swishing and swooshing and rippling up and down.

There's a swirling, whirling dragon, weaving to and fro,
Prancing and dancing and putting on a show.

There's cheering and clapping as the dragon draws near –
A sign of good luck and a happy new year!

John Foster

CARNIVAL

The festival of carnival is celebrated in February in many countries and began hundreds of years ago in Christian countries where Roman Catholicism was the dominant faith. Every year before the forty days of Lent – a time of fasting and repentance – began, Roman Catholics were given two days of feasting, dancing and merrymaking and this became known as the festival of Carnival. The word carnival comes from the Latin 'carne vale' which means farewell to flesh and in some countries it is still the custom to use up every scrap of meat, including the fat, to make pies and pastries.

Shrove Tuesday, the Tuesday before Lent, was a day for special feasting and it is still celebrated in some form in most European countries. In Britain we know it as Pancake Day. In France (as well as parts of North and South America) it is known as Mardi Gras, meaning 'Fat Tuesday' and when French people immigrated to the West Indies they took the festivities there. To begin with only the French people took part but before long the celebrations began to involve the Afro-Caribbean people and when slavery was abolished in the West Indies, Mardi Gras became a new kind of festival of the freed people. At first the European costumes were copied but these were quickly adapted and nowadays any kind of fancy dress is acceptable, the more exotic the better.

The most famous Carnival now takes place in Trinidad and Tobago and for a few days each year there is a fantastic spectacle and everywhere is alive with dancing, music-making and fantastically colourful processions.

Everybody loves carnival night

Music and adaptation of words by Art Podell

Carnival

Ev-ery-bo - dy   loves   Car -ni-val Night.

2. Everybody loves Carnival Night,
Everybody loves Carnival Night,
Everybody, everybody, everybody, everybody,
Everybody loves Carnival Night.

3. Masquerade and dance on Carnival Night,
Masquerade and dance on Carnival Night,
Everybody, everybody, everybody, everybody,
Masquerade and dance on Carnival Night.

4. Beat the pans and sing on Carnival Night,
Beat the pans and sing on Carnival Night,
Everybody, everybody, everybody, everybody,
Beat the pans and sing on Carnival Night.

Harlequin's new suit

'Everyone is going to wear special clothes,' Harlequin said to his mother, as he described the arrangements for Carnival. She shook her head sadly.

'And where are we going to get special clothes for you?' she asked. 'Things are so tight this year; there isn't a penny to spare.' Harlequin looked disappointed for a moment and then he spoke.

'Never mind, Mother. I can still go to the Carnival. I don't really need new clothes.'

A neighbour overheard that conversation between Harlequin and his mother. 'Do you know?' she said to her daughter. 'They can't afford a new Carnival suit for Harlequin this year.' The daughter went to look in her wardrobe. There was a lovely frill of red material which she had cut off a dress which was too long.

'I wonder whether Harlequin would like a red belt to brighten up his old suit?' she said.

When she went to the market next morning, the neighbour mentioned Harlequin's problem to the woman who kept the cheese stall. 'Do you know?' she said. 'They can't afford a new Carnival suit for Harlequin.' The cheese stall lady shook her head but, when she went home, she opened her dress-making drawer and pulled out a remnant of blue cotton.

'I wonder if this would be any good to Harlequin?' she thought.

At a dance that evening she mentioned Harlequin's problem to her partner, who happened to be a tailor. 'Do you know?' she said. 'They can't afford a new Carnival suit for Harlequin this year.' Her partner frowned and nearly stepped on her toes.

'Goodness me! I wish I could help, but the only spare material I have got in my workroom at the moment is a piece of yellow lining.'

His partner pulled him out of the dance and began to whisper in his ear. 'You've got some yellow material. I've got some blue squares. Jean has a red frill. Why don't we give them to Harlequin's mother? She could make him a lovely costume with patches of material in different colours. It would look splendid.'

At last the day of the Carnival came. The proudest boy there was Harlequin. 'Look!' he said. 'This was a present from my friend on the cheese stall.' He pointed to a blue square on his sleeve. 'Look at the red diamonds! They were a gift from my friend next door.' Everyone looked on admiringly as Harlequin spun round and round in the dance, as the Carnival procession went down the street.

Dorothy J. Taylor

The carnival

Steel bands practise out of sight,
In secret musicians play each night,
Through the villages the rumours abound,
The Carnival Calypso has now been found.

All is prepared for this special day,
When Trinidad's Carnival comes this way,
Colourful headdresses worn by the girls,
High on their heads and patterned with pearls.

Fantastic creatures of wire are made,
They disguise the people who join the parade,
Worked from behind, their limbs move about,
'Look, now they're coming,' everyone shouts.

A paper crocodile moves with the throng,
Covering the children who trundle along,
The pans gaily painted are wheeled through the street,
Come dance in the procession and lift up your feet.

Janet E. Greenyer

Play mas, Hannah

Hannah saw the costume as soon as she opened her eyes.

'OooooH!' Her mouth formed an 'O' as she gazed at it in wonder.

It was the costume of a lotus flower and Hannah was going to wear it for the competition. Every year at Carnival time there was a parade of children dressed in costumes at a large park called the Savannah. Hannah would dance and play mas on the stage so that everyone could see her lovely costume.

Mum came into the room and saw Hannah holding the skirt against her body.

'It's pretty, eh Hannah? Granny brought it last night when you were asleep.'

'Mum, d'you think it will fit me? Can I try it on *now*?' pleaded Hannah.

'Hannah, it's your Granny who made it you know, so it's sure to be alright. You must make haste with your b and b, *then* we'll see about trying it on.'

Mum always called Hannah's morning bath and breakfast her 'b and b'. It was a joke they shared.

'Now it's dressing-up time,' Mum said to Hannah when she had finished her breakfast.

Hannah was so excited she couldn't stand still. She hopped from one leg to the other.

'Child, if you can't stand still, I can't put on your costume. And NO costume, NO parade!' Mum said firmly.

So Hannah stood still.

First Mum put on Hannah's socks and a pair of new shoes. The shoes felt soft and light on her feet. The tops were made of coarse black canvas but they had rubber soles.

'Just the thing to jump in,' said Mum.

Next Mum put on the light blue blouse with hand-painted flowers around the neck and down the front.

Then Mum put on the dark blue satin skirt. There was an underskirt that made the whole thing stand out firm and stiff around Hannah. The skirt came right down to her ankles. Granny had shaped leaves from pieces of green and yellow cloth and sewn them around the hem of the skirt.

Last of all Mum put a stiff broad belt around Hannah's waist and fastened it with large safety pins. The belt was covered with pink petals which Hannah and her cousins had helped Auntie Liz to make. Mum spent a long time shaping the petals. She pointed them up and down, and this way and that way.

Hannah began to fidget again. 'Oh Mum, we'll never get to the parade on time,' she grumbled.

'Hannah, *please* be patient for a little longer. I want these to look like real petals.'

And Hannah stood still for a little longer.

At last Mum held Hannah a little way from her and looked her over.

'*I* want to see how it looks on me,' begged Hannah.

Mum took her to the living room and placed her in front of a full-length mirror.

'Look at yo'self, you lovely masquerade lady!' said Mum, and she spun Hannah round and round.

Hannah gazed at the girl in the mirror who didn't look a bit like her. She took off the skirt for Mum to put in a large plastic bag and Mum gave her a pair of denim trousers to wear until they got to the Savannah.

'Do you think Daddy will get away from work in time to see me parade?' asked Hannah, anxiously.

'If Daddy has to fly he will be there to see you play mas on the stage,' Mum promised.

Soon they were on their way to collect Granny.

The road around the Savannah was like a carpet of many colours. There were bands of children in costume everywhere. They filled the road and the pavements. In the midday heat coconut vendors were selling water-coconuts from trucks. The cool coconut water and soft sweet jelly satisfied hunger and thirst.

The air was alive with sounds – the toot-ti-toot of trumpets, the gentle strumming of guitars, the shic-shac of the maracas, and the ping-pong of steel drums.

A band of children in crisp, white sailor suits and bird-shaped headpieces chipped and swayed to the tune of a calypso. Even the youngest child in the band knew the words of the chorus:

'Ah feelin' hot, hot, hot
Ah feelin' hot, hot, hot...'

The calypso was on an audio tape and the music came from a truck fitted with loud-speakers. Someone had turned up the volume and it drowned out all the other sounds.

Hannah felt as though someone was pounding with a hammer inside her head and the world began to spin.

'Granny,' she said in a small voice, 'I feel sick.'

Granny put her hands on Hannah's face. It was flushed and her forehead was hot. Mum went to buy some coconuts and Granny lead Hannah away from the noise. They sat on the grass in the shade of a tree and Granny took Hannah in her arms and rocked her gently from side to side. She didn't say a word, just rocked Hannah.

After a while Hannah felt a cool breeze blowing around her face. It melted the hot ache inside her head.

Mum came back with three water-coconuts. One for each of them. The cool drink soothed Hannah. Not just her throat. She felt better deep inside her.

'I think I'm alright now,' she announced.

Granny said to Hannah, 'You know how we dance when you come to visit me?'

Hannah nodded. 'Granny could we dance together?' Hannah thought her Granny was the best dancer in the world and she loved to dance with her.

'Why not!' said Granny. 'Let's show Mum how well you can play mas with all those fancy dance steps.'

They moved closer to the stage where a small band of musicians were playing a lively tune. The stage was crowded with children. Some of them were disguised as rats, and a very tall masquerader in a pair of black tights and yellow jacket danced among the crowd of children and 'rats'. Everyone on the stage was dancing to the music and Hannah wanted to dance with them.

'Now let us play mas, Hannah!' said Granny.

Hannah and Granny danced to the music. Granny moved her feet to the right, then to the left. She spun half-way around to the right, then she spun half-way to the left. And Hannah did the same, clicking her fingers the way Granny did. Granny held both hands in the air and waved them from side to side. And all the time her feet made little steps to the right and to the left, backwards and forwards. And whatever Granny did, Hannah did.

'Smile, Hannah!' Mum called. 'Enjoy yo'self child!' And soon Hannah was enjoying herself so much she didn't notice a small group of people gathering round her.

'See, Hannah, there's nothing to worry about,' said Granny. 'When you go on stage just pretend you are dancing with me.'

'But Granny, supposin' I don't win the competition?'

'Hannah, when you get on that stage I want you to enjoy yourself. Dance all around the stage so that everyone can see your costume. But remember that Carnival is to enjoy!'

Just then they heard the announcer calling the names of the children who were to appear on stage. Hannah's was one of them.

'Come on, Hannah. Let's get the rest of your costume on,' said Mum. She hurried Hannah off to a tent to change.

Granny was waiting for them outside the tent and they headed for the stage entrance. A little girl dressed in the costume of a Japanese doll was just going off stage in a flurry of gold and red and blue silk.

'Mum, Granny, that's Mylin from our school. Her Mum made the costume,' whispered Hannah. The costume was so beautiful that there were lots of photographers trying to get pictures of Mylin as her mother helped her off stage.

The crowd in the stand were still applauding Mylin when a large spider landed on the floor right in the middle of the stage. The 'spider' was really a very tall boy covered from head to toe in a costume of shiny black material covered with fine black feathers. There were two extra pairs of legs, one joined at his waist and the other under his arms. When he crawled on the floor he looked like a real spider and every time he leaped and spun around on his toes, a long length of fine silky material unwound from somewhere on his body. Across the back of his costume the words 'ANANCY STORY' were painted in silver. He danced around the stage once, twice, then as suddenly as he had appeared, he leaped off the stage and was gone.

Now it was Hannah's turn.

She heard someone call her name.

Mum kissed her and whispered, 'Remember, enjoy!'

Someone came and took her hand and led her on to the stage. She looked around for Mum and Granny but she couldn't see them anywhere. There were too many people. The music sounded far away. And there was a buzzing noise in her ears. She wanted to move but she couldn't.

Then she heard a voice saying, 'Mummy, that's my friend Hannah. She's the best dancer in our class!' She saw hands waving and a friendly voice calling, 'Hannah! It's me, Karen!'

Hannah heard the music now, clearly, and she wanted to dance. She wanted to dance so well that Karen would be proud of her. She wanted everyone to enjoy themselves too. She began to dance around the stage to show her costume. She danced the way Granny showed her but as she began to enjoy herself she made up her own steps. She spun like Anancy the spider, and she jumped. She swayed and shook her shoulders, and all the time she smiled at the crowd.

She heard Granny's voice, 'Play mas, Hannah!'

Then a chorus of voices calling, 'Play mas, Hannah!'

And Hannah did some of the twirls and turns that Granny had taught her. The crowd clapped and danced with her. They whooped and whistled at her and she danced faster and faster until the music slid to a stop.

The announcer was saying '...and as much as we would like to keep this wonderful dancer on stage we must move on....' But Hannah didn't hear the rest for she was lifted off the stage. It was Hannah's Dad. He had arrived in time to see her parade on stage and play mas.

'Hannah, that was fantastic,' said Dad, his face beaming.

Mum and Granny hugged her.

'We're so proud of you, Hannah!' said Granny.

'Were you frightened?' Mum asked.

'Only at first, but afterwards I enjoyed it so much I didn't want it to end. Mum, can I play mas again next Carnival?'

Mum laughed. 'Hannah! Hannah!' she said. 'You're a true mas lady now!'

Grace Hallworth

Carnival

David Moses

mu - sic played,   To the con - ga beat.   Makes you   dance,   makes you

sway,   Makes you   feel on ho - li - day,   when   it's

To end, repeat the chorus ad lib and fade

2. No matter where you are,
It's time for Mardi Gras.
Have some fun, winter's done,
Summer can't be far.
So let's dance, and let's sway
And let's have a holiday, now it's –

Chorus

3. Pushing through the press
Nobody can guess
Who you are behind your mask
Wearing fancy dress.
So you dance, and you sway,
And enjoy the holiday, now it's –

Chorus

4. Lanterns burning bright
Shining in the night,
Candles flicker, torches blaze,
Everywhere there's light.
And we dance, and we sway,
and enjoy our holiday, when it's –

Chorus

Shrove Tuesday

When I came home on Tuesday
feeling ever so hungry,
my Dad was in the kitchen
making pancakes for our tea.

Into half a pound of flour,
he mixed a pint of milk,
cracked eggs into the batter
and beat it smooth as silk.

Next he took the frying pan
and heated drops of oil.
Until the pan was sizzling,
we waited for a while.

Soon everything was ready.
Dad poured batter in the pan
but when we turned it over
– *then* the fun began.

Dad offered me the frying pan.
'Toss that pancake in the air!'
With both hands on the handle,
I took my aim with care.

The pancake somersaulted.
It flipped around and round.
When it flopped into the pan,
it had turned up golden brown!

We sat and ate our pancakes,
remembering what it meant.
Tomorrow it's Ash Wednesday,
that's the start of Lent.

Chris Riley

PURIM

Purim, a Jewish festival, is called after the word *pur*, meaning 'lots' or dice (which Haman cast) and falls on the 14th of Adar (February or March) each year. This was the day Haman chose for the Jews to be killed, and thus it celebrates the deliverance of the Jews from a wicked, destructive plot.

The day prior to Purim is a fast day, the Fast of Esther, and the festival centres around the reading of the story of Esther, Mordecai and Haman found in the Book of Esther. This book is written on a scroll called the Megillah and is read on the evening before and on the morning of the festival day in synagogues and homes. Every time the name Haman is read, the children in the congregation boo, hiss, stamp their feet and shake their greggers (rattles) to try to drown out his evil name.

Children dress in fancy dress and families share a festive meal. Presents are given and gifts of money sent to the poor.

A special sticky, three-cornered cake or biscuit filled with poppy seeds, called hamantaschen, is eaten. This is supposed to look like Haman's ears, or hat, some say.

Getting ready for Purim

'What are you making, Mummy?' Sara climbed up to the kitchen stool beside her mother as she asked the question. Mother took her hands out of the mixing bowl and reached for the jug of water.

'Pastry,' she replied. 'Pastry for hamantaschen.' Sara leant over to dip her finger in the bowl of brown filling.

'I like hamantaschen,' she said. 'What do you put in the filling?'

Her mother smiled: 'Prunes, walnuts, sugar, lemon juice – and if you steal any more there won't be enough left for the hamantaschen.'

Sara licked her finger. 'Why do we call them hamantaschen?' she said.

'I told you the story last year at Purim,' replied her mother. 'Once upon a time there was a beautiful girl called Esther and she was a queen.'

'Oh, yes, I remember,' said Sara. 'She was married to King Ahasuerus and had a cousin who wanted her help.'

'That's right,' said Sara's mother. 'The nasty Haman was planning to kill all Esther's people – the Jews who had settled in Persia.'

Sara was quiet for a moment, remembering the story. She took another lick of prune filling, which had fallen on the table while her mother was filling the pastry circles 'And we eat hamantaschen to remind us of that nasty Haman. We chew him all up,' she went on, with a giggle. Then she jumped off the stool. 'I remember the noise we made in the synagogue,' she said. 'We clapped our hands and stamped our feet every time Haman's name was read. The big children swung their greggers. Oh, Mummy, can I make a gregger this year?'

When the hamantaschen were in the oven, Sara and her mother turned their attention to the making of a gregger. It was easy to find an empty plastic bottle, but what would make the best rattle? 'Try some dried beans,' said Sara's mother, but their sound was not loud enough for Sara. 'What about some nuts in their shells?' suggested Mother, but Sara could not get them through the little hole.

'I know,' said Sara, 'I'll get some pebbles from the garden.' Before the hamantaschen were out of the oven, the gregger was ready.

'Now for a practice,' said Mother. 'Every time I say Haman, shake your gregger.' Sara held it ready. 'Once upon a time, long ago, there was a wicked courtier called....' And no one heard the name, because Sara's gregger made such a loud noise.

'Hurrah for Purim,' she shouted, and Mother dashed to the oven to get out the hamantaschen.

Dorothy J. Taylor

Baking a Hamantash

Pat-a-cake, Pat-a-cake,
Baker's man,
Bake me a Hamantash
Fast as you can!
Roll it, and fold it,
And make corners three;
Make one for mommy, for daddy and me!
Pat-a-cake, Pat-a-cake,
Nice baker's man,
Bake me a Hamantash
Fast as you can!

Sara G. Levy

Purim

Purim am I, Purim am I,
All goodness and good cheer,
But only once a year do I
Come visiting you here.
Hooray Purim, Hooray Purim,
Drums beat and cymbals chime,
Oh what a shame the feast can't last
For one or two month's time!

Traditional Jewish song

My name is Purim

Traditional Jewish

At a moderate pace

1. My name is Pu - rim and I come, Great fun and fro - lic bring - ing. Just once a year I vi - sit you To cheer you with my sing - ing. La la la la la la la la la la la la la la la la la la la la la.

2. Hurrah Purim! Hurrah Purim!
I love your merry drumming
And if I had my way, Purim,
Each month you would be coming.

Chorus

3. Oh, Mr Purim tell us why
We see you only yearly?
Please make it once or twice a week
Because we love you dearly.

Chorus

The story of Purim

Many, many years ago in the country that was once called Persia there lived a king named Ahasuerus. One day he called to his wife, Queen Vashti but she did not answer him. King Ahasuerus was furious because he expected to be obeyed, and by his wife of all people. So he decided to punish Vashti; he would send her away and find a new queen instead. An announcement was made: 'King Ahasuerus will choose a new wife from all the beautiful young girls in the land.'

Now in Ahasuerus' kingdom there was a Jewish man whose name was Mordecai. He had a beautiful young niece called Esther. The King's soldiers made his command known to Esther and she was troubled, but Mordecai told her to make ready to be seen by the King though on no account must she let it be known that she was Jewish.

King Ahasuerus was enchanted by Esther's beauty and dignity and chose her for his wife and soon after she became Queen.

Then one day while he was standing at the palace gates waiting to see Esther, Mordecai overheard some of the guards plotting to kill King Ahasuerus. So he told his niece of the plot. Esther informed the King who promised Mordecai a reward for his good deed.

Among those who gained favour with the King was a man called Haman; he became his Chief Minister and everyone was expected to bow before him. When Mordecai refused to bow, Haman was furious and set about finding out all he could about the man. When he found out that Mordecai was a Jew, Haman was filled with hatred, not only for him but for all Jewish people. He plotted to kill Mordecai and all the other Jews too.

Haman went to King Ahasuerus and said, 'There is a race of people living in this kingdom; people who do not obey the law of the land. They should be destroyed.' Such was Ahasuerus' trust in Haman that he began to worry about this. Meanwhile Haman continued plotting and he cast lots to decide on a date for the destruction of the Jews.

Eventually he drew a lot which told him the time was right to act so he went again and reminded the King once more about the people causing trouble in his kingdom. Such was Ahasuerus' trust in Haman that he gave him permission to do whatever he thought best. So Haman ordered notices to be posted in every market place in the land proclaiming that on the 13th of the 12th month every Jew, whether man, woman or child, was to be killed.

Now when Mordecai learned of the wicked plan he dressed himself in sackcloth and ashes and went and stood outside the palace gates. Esther saw him and wondered what was the matter, so she called one of her servants and sent him to find out. Mordecai gave him a copy of the written decree ordering the destruction of the Jews and instructed him to show it to Esther and beg her to go to the King and plead with him to save the Jewish people and, of course, herself.

It was the custom that no one, not even Queen Esther, was allowed to go to the King unless he called for them; the punishment for disobeying was death. So Esther prepared herself for the meeting by praying to God and fasting. She also sent word that Mordecai and all the Jews should do the same. After three days, summoning her courage, Esther went to the King and invited him and Haman to a feast on the following day. Meanwhile Haman had ordered a gallows to be built on which to hang Mordecai; this would put him in a good mood for the feast, he thought.

That night the King had difficulty sleeping and passed the time by ordering a reading of the court records. On hearing Mordecai's name he remembered the promise of a reward to the Jew who had saved his life. In the morning he called Haman saying, 'How should I reward a man who has pleased me?'

Haman, believing that the King was referring to him, replied, 'Cloth him in royal dress, mount him on one of the King's horses and let the people cheer him through the streets.'

'Very well,' said King Ahasuerus, 'See to it that Mordecai the Jew who saved my life receives this treatment.' The furious Haman had to agree.

At the feast Haman's anger increased still further when the King offered the Queen a favour. 'Give me my life and that of my people,' begged Esther and then explained that she was a Jew and that Haman had tricked him into believing that the Jews were making their own laws. King Ahasuerus loved his wife so much that he agreed to her request and ordered that Haman be hung on the gallows that had been set up for Mordecai. So all the Jews were spared.

As a reminder that they were saved, Jewish people feast and celebrate on the 14th day of Adar. They exchange gifts and the story of Esther is read in synagogues. On the day before Purim is celebrated Jewish people fast in memory of how Esther prepared herself before she went to the King.

Colin J. Bennett

Purim

Read the Book of Esther.
Hear again the news
Of how the wicked Haman
Plotted against the Jews.

Read again how Mordechai
Stood in Haman's way;
Of how the lot was drawn
To choose his execution day.

Read how good Queen Esther
Pleaded for her race;
How Mordechai was saved
And Haman took his place.

As you hear the story
Of the evil man's defeat,
Drown out his wicked name
With the stamping of your feet.

John Foster

Purim

The Jews remember a life filled with fear,
When the Festival of Purim comes around each year,
Hanman, a member of the Persian court,
Hated the Jews and their destruction sought.

All because Mordecaih had withheld his respect,
Which Hanman, a courtier, had come to expect,
So he persuaded the King that the Jews he should kill,
And then with their money his pockets he'd fill.

But the Persian King had a Jewish wife,
Who had been fostered by Mordecaih most of her life,
The King spoke to her kindly, 'Do all you can,'
'To save the Jews from this wicked man.'

So she called all her servants, 'Now a banquet prepare,'
Then invited Hanman to savour the fayre,
Graciously she helped the strong wine to find,
Knowing its influence would weaken his mind.

Now Esther, the King's wife, is revered to this day,
For she saved her people and this fear did allay,
So children now dress up as Kings and Queens,
And act out the story and learn what it means.

Janet E. Greenyer

HOLI

Holi, the Hindu spring festival of colour, is celebrated on the day when there is a full moon in the month of Phalgun (February–March). It is one of India's oldest festivals and many legends and stories are associated with it.

One story tells that the festival is named after Holika, sister of the demon king, Hiranyakashipu. He was furious because his son, Prahlad, refused to worship him as a god and so he asked his sister (who it is said, could not be burnt by fire) to sit on a burning pyre holding Prince Prahlad. Holika agreed but died in the fire whereas Prahlad was unhurt.

To mark the death of Holika, huge bonfires are lit on the eve of Holi – Holika Dahan – songs are sung around the fire and coconuts are roasted over it and shared. The fire represents the triumph of good over evil.

In some parts of India people erect a dried tree trunk a month before and then on the day of Holika Dahan the whole community gathers there and dried grass is heaped around the tree trunk. Nowadays crackers will also be added to the pile. The head of the community sets the heap alight. The farmers bring wheat grains and chickpeas and roast them in the fire. These are shared as prashad. All the children born during the year participate in a ceremony. The parents, with their baby, sit in front of the fire and perform a puja ceremony. They then walk around the fire seven times holding the baby. This is intended to protect the child from evil.

On the day of the festival people throw coloured powders or water at each other. They are said to 'play Dhulandi', which is based on a story about Krishna. It is a time of tricks, fun and dancing. In some parts of India Holi is also a harvest celebration.

Radha and Krishna play Holi

Lord Krishna lived in India a long, long time ago. When he was a young boy Krishna often got into all kinds of mischief and as he got older his pranks increased. He loved to tease the milkmaids – the gopis – and even took all their clothes while they were bathing in the River Yamuna one day.

Now Krishna had a special friend, a beautiful girl named Radha. She and Krishna and lots of their friends liked to dance and play games on the banks of the Yamuna, and Krishna often played his flute to entertain them.

One full moon night in early spring the gopis came to dance. In their

brightly coloured clothes they twirled to the sound of Krishna's flute. When they heard the sweet music many more people came to dance.

All at once Krishna put down his flute and disappeared. He was soon back carrying some pots, each containing a coloured powder. He put the pots down and called, 'Radha, Radha, see what I've got.' Radha left the other dancers and ran towards him. Then suddenly Krishna took a handful of red powder and threw it at her, then some green and some yellow. Soon Radha was covered in coloured powder. She took hold of one of the pots and began to throw powder back at Krishna. By now everyone had stopped dancing and come over to watch the fun. Before long everyone started to join in and coloured powder was flying everywhere. The air was filled with colour and noisy laughter.

From that time on, every springtime, Holi is celebrated when people throw coloured powder or water at each other as a joyful reminder of the fun Krishna and his friends had long ago.

Renuka Singh

Holi

Light the festive bonfire.
Watch the flames leap high.
See the demon's spirit
Fly into the sky.

Tomorrow will be Holi.
We'll laugh, dance and sing
And throw our coloured powders
To welcome in the spring.

John Foster

A blind girl celebrates Holi

I cannot see
The new crimson sari
My aunt has sent me,
But I can feel its softness,
Run my fingers along
Its silver edge,
I see the bonfire's
Red and yellow flames,
I hear their fizz and crackle
And the cries of the people
Throwing paint and water,
Soaking each other in colour!
I can smell the roasted coconuts
And taste the popcorn
The dates and lentils,
Holi is red and gold,
Fire and spice,
The festival of colours!

Theresa Heine

Holi

'Right, children, it's time to start work, so settle down please.' Miss Drummond closed the register and looked around the classroom. 'We're going to be talking about something very exciting today, and I've even got a surprise for you! So get out your notebooks and pencils. Quietly, please.'

Trying hard not to laugh, Ajay watched Sarika from his desk in the corner. At that moment she was chatting to her best friend Emma who sat next to her. But in just about two seconds flat when she opened her desk to get her notebook and pencil out, Sarika Sharma was going to get the biggest shock of her life! And Ajay could hardly wait to see what happened.

It was about time he got his own back on Sarika, he thought gleefully. The week before, Sarika had sneaked into the cloakroom, and filled his plimsolls with water. Ajay had only found out just before a games lesson, and he'd had to run around the gym in wet, squelchy shoes that made a rude noise every time he put his foot down. Sarika had said she was only getting her own back because the week before THAT, Ajay had put bubblegum on the seat of her chair, and it had stuck to her bottom. But Ajay had only put bubblegum on Sarika's chair because the week before THAT, she'd stuffed grass down the back of his neck when they were out in the playground. And the week before THAT – but Ajay couldn't remember what had happened the week before that. He and Sarika had played so many tricks on each other, he couldn't remember them all.

Ajay sat up eagerly in his chair as Sarika, still whispering to her friend Emma, began to open the lid of her desk. She opened it higher – and higher – and higher, and Ajay had to bite his lip to stop himself from squeaking with laughter. Quickly he nudged his best mate Dennis, who was sitting next to him, hard in the ribs.

'Ow!' grumbled Dennis crossly, wrinkling his freckled nose. 'What was that for?'

'Watch this!' Ajay whispered, grinning from ear to ear.

Sarika was just reaching inside her desk to look for her notebook and pencil. And then –

'EEEEEEK! HELP!' Sarika leapt to her feet, and let out an ear-splitting scream that nearly made the whole class jump out of its skin. 'Miss! There's a spider in my desk!'

'What?' Miss Drummond was so startled, she leapt up out of her own chair too.

'There's a spider in my desk, Miss!' Sarika shouted, her eyes wide with fear. 'It's big and black and hairy and – and it ran under my maths book!'

The rest of the class started to giggle, and Ajay laughed so hard his sides ached. He'd really shown old Bossyboots Sharma this time, he thought triumphantly. Served her right for putting water in his plimsolls!

'Calm down, Sarika,' said Miss Drummond. 'It won't hurt you.'

'I HATE spiders!' wailed Sarika. 'Get it out of my desk, quick, Emma!'

'It's probably more frightened than you are, Sarika,' said Miss Drummond as Emma reached into the open desk, gently scooped the

work, children,' she said sternly.

Ajay and Sarika's class had been doing a topic on spring for the last few weeks now, and the children were enjoying the work they'd been doing very much. They'd made a frieze of the school playground, showing how different it looked in winter to spring, when all the trees and flowers started blossoming again. Miss Drummond had told them all about how plants started to grow again in the spring, and the children had planted daffodil bulbs in pots. Every day they measured them to see how much they'd grown, and of course, Ajay and Sarika were always arguing over whose daffodil was the biggest. Dennis had even brought his tortoise Oscar into school. Oscar had been asleep all through the winter, and Miss Drummond had told the children all about hibernation, and how some animals go to sleep all winter, and wake up again in the spring.

'Miss,' said Sarika eagerly, 'You said you'd got a surprise for us today. What is it?'

'Well,' said Miss Drummond with a smile, 'We've got a very special visitor coming to see us, and he should be here any minute now.' And right at that very moment there was a knock at the classroom door.

All the children looked round curiously. The door opened, and a short, plump man with twinkling dark eyes and almost no hair at all came in.

'That's Mr Choudhury from the corner shop!' said Ajay.

The children stared at each other in surprise. They all knew Mr Choudhury. They went to his shop every day after school to buy ice-cream and sweets and comics. But what was he doing here, in their classroom?

spider up in her hand and carried it over to the door. 'I wonder how it got inside your desk in the first place....'

Ajay stopped laughing and tried to look as innocent as he could as Miss Drummond stared at him hard. She knew very well that he and Sarika were always playing tricks on each other, and if the teacher asked him if he'd put the spider in Sarika's desk, he'd have to say yes. But luckily for him, Miss Drummond wanted to get on with the lesson.

'I think we've wasted quite enough time. Notebooks and pencils out, please.'

Ajay breathed a sigh of relief. But, as Miss Drummond went back to her table, Sarika swung round and shot him a furious glare.

'Very funny, Ajay Patel!' she mouthed at him. 'I know it was you. You're in big trouble!'

Ajay opened his mouth to say something back, then shut it again as he noticed that Miss Drummond was looking at him again.

'Time we got on with some topic

'Mr Choudhury's very kindly come into school to help us with our topic on spring, children,' Miss Drummond explained. 'He's going to tell you all about a very special festival that takes place in India every springtime.'

'Yes,' said Mr Choudhury with a smile. 'When I was a little boy in India, and that wasn't so VERY long ago...' the children giggled '...the spring was always a very happy time for us, because that's when we celebrated Holi.'

'Holi?' said Dennis. 'What's that?'

Miss Drummond wrote Holi on the board. It was spelt H-O-L-I.

'Holi is the time when people in India celebrate the coming of spring and the gathering of the wheat harvest,' Mr Choudhury explained. 'And the first thing you kids need to know about Holi is that it's FUN! In India, the children love Holi as much as you love Christmas.'

'Why?' asked the children.

'Ah, because at Holi, the children are allowed to do WHATEVER they like!' laughed Mr Choudhury. 'Shall I tell you what happens?'

'Yes, please!' said the class, looking interested.

'Well, first of all,' said Mr Choudhury, 'a few days before Holi, me and my brothers and sisters would go out and buy lots of different coloured powders. Then we'd mix them up with water until we'd made lots of beautiful colours. Reds, golds, blues, greens and purples. And then do you know what everybody did when Holi came along?' He looked round at the children. 'We all went out into the streets, and we threw coloured water and red powder everywhere, all over each other, and over anyone else who happened to come along too, so we all ended up soaked to the skin, and covered in lots and lots of different colours like a rainbow!'

The children started giggling. Holi sounded like brilliant fun to them!

'We kept the most beautiful and special colours for our friends,' Mr Choudhury went on. 'And it wasn't just the children either. All the grown-ups joined in too, and we were allowed to throw coloured water over anyone we liked!'

'What, even your TEACHERS?' asked Ajay, his eyes round with surprise.

'Yes, even our teachers!'

chuckled Mr Choudhury. 'Because EVERYONE has to join in and enjoy the fun at Holi.'

'Didn't you get told off?' asked Dennis.

Mr Choudhury shook his head. 'No,' he said. 'Everyone plays tricks on each other at Holi, but nobody gets into trouble!'

'Yes, we know all about tricks in THIS class,' said Miss Drummond, looking at Ajay and Sarika. 'What else happens at Holi, Mr Choudhury?'

'Well, everyone comes out into the street, and there's loud music and lots of dancing and we light bonfires too,' said Mr Choudhury, 'People believe that Holi's a good time to forgive anyone who's behaved badly towards you. So everyone tries to be friendly to each other.'

'My granny's told me about Holi,' said Sarika. 'I wish we had Holi in England.'

'So do I,' said Dennis. 'It sounds brilliant!'

'Well...,' Miss Drummond looked round at the class. 'How about if, tomorrow afternoon, we have our very own Holi festival, right here in the playground?'

The children's mouths fell open in amazement.

'Really, Miss?' asked Ajay. 'With coloured water and everything?'

Miss Drummond nodded.

'It's going to be good fun, but very messy too. So you'd better wear your oldest clothes tomorrow!'

The children burst out talking and giggling all at once, they were so excited. Their own Holi festival, right here in the playground!

'It's going to be a real laugh!' Sarika's friend Emma said to her. 'I can't wait till tomorrow!'

'Neither can I,' said Sarika with a wicked grin. 'You heard what Mr Choudhury said about people playing tricks at Holi? Well, tomorrow Ajay Patel's going to be really, really, REALLY sorry he put that spider in my desk!'

Early next morning, the children in Miss Drummond's class were hard at work. Miss Drummond had given them lots of different coloured paints, and they were busy mixing up the most beautiful colours they could make. Mr Choudhury had come back into school to help them, and he'd brought in a big box full of empty washing-up liquid bottles, so that the coloured water could be put inside them, ready for the Holi festival in the playground that afternoon.

'Remember, children, don't use too much paint, or it will be too thick and make a terrible mess,' warned Miss Drummond. 'Mix in plenty of water.'

'That's nice colour,' said Emma to Sarika. Sarika had mixed up a beautiful deep red and was pouring it carefully into a squeezy bottle. 'Promise you'll squirt that one all over me!'

'Oh, I will' said Sarika. 'But I've got something else too. Look.' She lowered her voice and looked round to check that Miss Drummond was safely over the other side of the room. Then she opened her desk and took out another squeezy bottle.

'What's that?' asked Emma.

'This is a special colour, just for people named Ajay!' Sarika giggled. She tipped the bottle upside-down carefully, and squeezed it very gently on to the newspaper that covered her desk. Thick, lumpy, dirty-grey oozed out with a gloop-gloop sound.

'Yuk!' said Emma. 'You'd better put some water in and mix it up, or

Miss Drummond will tell you off.'

Sarika shook her head.

'I'm going to get my own back on Ajay Patel for putting that spider in my desk yesterday.' She winked at Emma. 'He won't be laughing when he's covered in lumpy grey paint!'

'And you won't be laughing when Miss Drummond gives you a detention,' said Emma with a sigh. 'I wish you and Ajay would stop playing tricks on each other. Why can't you just be friends?'

'He started it,' said Sarika with a sniff, and she put the bottle carefully back into her desk. But what she didn't know was that Ajay was watching her across the classroom.

'Sarika Sharma's up to something!' he said furiously to Dennis. 'Did you see that squeezy bottle she just hid in her desk?'

'What?' Dennis wasn't taking much notice. He was carefully adding white paint to blue and seeing what sort of colour he could get.

'I just bet I know what's in that bottle too!' Ajay muttered angrily. 'I bet she's mixed up something really disgusting. Well, I'm going to be ready for her!'

He reached under the desk and showed Dennis the squeezy bottle he'd hidden under there.

'What's in it?' asked Dennis with a frown.

Ajay tipped the bottle upside-down and squeezed it gently. Thick, lumpy black paint oozed out with a gloop-gloop sound. Dennis shook his head.

'Miss Drummond's going to go mad if you use that,' he warned Ajay.

'Well, if Sarika's going to do it to me, I'm going to do it to her!' said Ajay crossly.

'I wish you and Sarika would stop playing tricks on each other,

and just be friends,' said Dennis with a sigh.

'She started it,' said Ajay with a sniff, and he put the bottle carefully on the floor under his desk.

Dennis gave up trying. Sarika and Ajay had been playing tricks on each other for years, and he was sure they were never, ever going to stop. He picked up his water pot, and went over to the sink to clean it out. Emma was already standing there, washing out her paintbrush.

'Hi, Dennis,' she said. 'Guess what? Sarika's mixed up a horrible, lumpy, grey paint and she's going to use it on Ajay when we have our Holi festival this afternoon.'

'Well, Ajay's got a horrible, lumpy, black paint and he's going to use it on Sarika,' sighed Dennis. 'Miss Drummond is going to go MAD.'

'I know. The whole afternoon's going to be spoilt,' said Emma, and she and Dennis stared gloomily at each other.

'What's going on here?' Mr Choudhury came up to them, beaming all over his face. 'Don't you remember what I told you about Holi, kids? It's FUN! So why are you looking so miserable?'

'It's Ajay and Sarika,' Dennis said. 'They're going to play a trick on each other this afternoon.'

'Well that's okay,' smiled Mr Choudhury. 'In India, friends often play tricks on each other at Holi.'

'But Ajay and Sarika aren't friends!' wailed Emma. 'And they don't just play tricks at Holi, they do it all the time! They're going to spoil everything this afternoon, and Miss Drummond's going to be really, really mad.'

Mr Choudhury thought for a moment or two. 'Do you remember me telling you yesterday that Holi was a good time for people to forget everything that had happened in the past, and make friends again?'

'Yeah,' said Dennis, 'But Ajay and Sarika will never, ever, ever be friends!'

'Well, maybe they secretly want to be friends, and they just need some help – and a bit of Holi

himself. Sometimes playing tricks on Sarika wasn't very much fun at all, not when he ended up with double detention.

'Ah, that looks a very nice colour you've mixed up there, Ajay.' Mr Choudhury had come over to the desk, and was standing watching

magic.' Mr Choudhury winked at Dennis and Emma. 'Listen, this is what I'm going to do....'

Back at his desk, Ajay hadn't noticed Dennis and Emma talking to Mr Choudhury. He was too busy adding gold paint to water, and trying to get the colour just right. As he mixed, Ajay thought about the Holi festival that afternoon. He was really looking forward to it – except that he was bound to get into trouble with Miss Drummond for spraying Sarika with that horrible black paint. Ajay sighed to

him. 'I expect you'll be using that on your friend, Sarika.'

'Sarika's not my friend!' squeaked Ajay indignantly.

'Oh?' Mr Choudhury looked puzzled. 'But she just told me she was your BEST friend! And she's made a beautiful dark red colour, just for you! She told me so herself!'

Ajay's mouth dropped open in amazement. 'But–but I put that spider in her desk yesterday!' he stammered. 'I thought she'd be out to get me!'

'Oh no.' Mr Choudhury shook his head. 'Sarika's forgotten all about that. She wants to be friends! So make sure you've got a special colour mixed up for her, won't you?'

Ajay was so shocked, he couldn't say a word as Mr Choudhury walked off. Sarika wanted to be friends with him! He could hardly believe it – especially after he'd put that spider in her desk. Ajay felt ashamed of himself. Well, if Sarika wanted to be friends, so did he. He was tired of playing tricks and getting into trouble all the time. Quickly he picked up the bottle of lumpy black paint that stood under his desk. He went over to the sink, and emptied the bottle out, washing all the black lumps away.

Meanwhile, Mr Choudhury had now gone over to talk to Sarika.

'I've just been chatting to Ajay,' said Mr Choudhury. 'And he told me he's mixed up a special colour just for you, Sarika.'

'Yeah, I BET he has!' said Sarika, flicking her long black plaits off her face. 'And I bet it's really horrible and disgusting! I hate him!'

'Oh no!' said Mr Choudhury. 'It's a beautiful golden colour. I'm sure you'll like it!'

Sarika's mouth fell open.

'WHAT?' she said.

'Ajay told me he was very sorry he put the spider in your desk, and he wants to be friends,' explained Mr Choudhury. 'Remember what I told you about Holi being a time when everybody should be friends again?'

Sarika was so amazed, she couldn't say a word. Ajay wanted to be friends with HER? She could hardly believe it. Especially after he'd put the spider in her desk. But after all, she'd been mean to HIM by filling his plimsolls with water... Sarika felt ashamed of

herself. Well, if Ajay wanted to be friends, so did she. She was tired of playing tricks and getting into trouble all the time. She opened her desk, took out the bottle of lumpy grey paint and went over to the sink. She tipped the bottle up, emptied it out and washed all the grey lumps away.

'See?' Mr Choudhury whispered to Dennis and Emma, 'All it needed was a bit of Holi magic!'

The spring sunshine was shining brightly that afternoon when bursting with excitement, Miss Drummond's class, wearing their oldest and shabbiest clothes, poured out into the playground for the start of their very own Holi festival. All the children had mixed up two or three different colours, and their arms were full of squeezy bottles.

'Right, children!' said Miss Drummond. 'When I blow the whistle, Holi begins!'

'Happy Holi!' shouted Mr Choudhury, who'd come to watch.

As soon as Miss Drummond blew her whistle, the children scattered out over the playground, screaming and laughing – and the next moment, a beautiful rainbow of lots of different colours shot up into the air as they aimed their squeezy bottles at their friends and let fly. Red, gold, blue, purple and green water glistened in the sunlight as showers of coloured drops cascaded everywhere like huge fountains.

'Look at me – I'm all blue!' shouted Emma, as Dennis caught her in a shower of sky-blue water and covered her from head to foot. She aimed her own bottle at Dennis as her ran off, and sprayed a stream of bright green water all over the back of the old shirt he was wearing.

'I get the feeling the children are enjoying Holi quite a bit!' said Mr Choudhury to Miss Drummond.

'Yes, I think they are!' Miss Drummond laughed, but then her smile faded. 'Oh no!' She looked across the playground to where Ajay and Sarika were taking aim at each other with their squeezy bottles.

"I hope Ajay and Sarika aren't going to spoil the afternoon by playing any nasty tricks on each other. Ajay! Sarika!'

Ajay and Sarika turned round as Miss Drummond came hurrying towards them.

'What's in those bottles, you two?' Miss Drummond asked suspiciously. 'Nothing horrible, I hope!'

'Course not, Miss!' Ajay said indignantly. 'I wouldn't do that to Sarika – she's my friend!'

'WHAT?' said Miss Drummond, looking as if she was about to faint with shock.

'And Ajay's MY friend, Miss!' said Sarika. 'I mixed up a special colour just for him!'

'I don't believe it – I just don't believe it! said Miss Drummond as she watched Ajay and Sarika shower each other with beautiful, glittering red and golden streams of water, and then run off together arm-in-arm, giggling their heads off. 'What on earth has happened to those two?'

'HOLI MAGIC, Miss Drummond!' shouted Dennis, Emma and Mr Choudhury. 'Happy Holi!'

Narinder Dhami

Holi with Shyam

Sujan Rawtani

(Shyam and Kanhiya are names for Lord Krishna and Radha.)

Holi – festival of spring

Holi is the Indian Spring Festival, a time when winter crops, such as wheat and mustard seeds, are harvested.

I cannot tell you how much I looked forward to this festival. In fact, I longed for it a good three hundred and sixty-four days of the year.

The reason was that our whole family did *such* unusual things to celebrate Holi.

First of all, on the day of the full moon around late February or early March, we built a huge bonfire. This was called 'burning Holi', because on this day, ages ago, a wicked princess, Holika, was consumed by flames that she had intended for her innocent nephew Prahlad.

Frankly, I cared less for Holika, who was burnt in ancient history, than I did for the stuff we actually threw into our own bonfire. We threw whole sheafs of green wheat, whole bundles of green chickpeas, still on their stalks, pinecones filled with strategically hidden pinenuts, and then watched them as their skins got charred.

Only the outside skins were allowed to burn. That was the trick. Each one of us then used a stick to pull out whatever we wanted to eat. My favourite was the chickpeas – tiny chickpeas still in their green skins. Of course, the skins would turn brownish-black but the peas themselves would be deliciously roasted. Everything would be hot – we would almost burn our fingers trying to peel the chickpeas and remove the shells from the pinenuts. Their taste would have to last us for the rest of the year as we licked our lips and remembered. By the end of it all, our faces were black and our clothes and hands were sooty, but no one seemed to mind, not even our parents.

The funny thing about Holi was that we could 'burn' it one night and 'play' it the next morning. While the 'burning' had to do, naturally, with fire, the 'playing' had to do with water and colours.

It was said that Lord Krishna, the blue god, played Holi with the milkmaids, so who were we to do any less?

As the Spring Festival approached, an army of us young cousins would, in great secrecy and in competing groups, begin its preparation of colours. At Holi, all Indians, of all ages, have the licence to rub or throw colours – water-based, oil-based or in powder form – on the victims of their choice. No one is considered worthy of exemption, dignified grandmothers included.

Holi is a leveller, and there was no one we wanted to level more than those against whom we held grudges. A special ugly colour was prepared for them.

First, we would go to the garage and call on one of the chauffeurs. 'Masoom Ali? Masoom Ali?' we would call.

Masoom Ali would poke his head out from the pit under the gleaming Ford. 'I am busy. Why are you children always disturbing me? Always coming here to eat my head. Barrister Sa'ab, your grandfather, wants the car at noon and I still have much work to do.'

'Just give us some of the dirtiest grease from under the car.'

'So, Holi is upon us again? Why don't you children use the normal red, green and yellow colours?'

'If you give us the grease, we won't spray you with the awful magenta paint we have prepared in the garden watertank. It is a fast colour too.'

'Threatening an old man, are you! All right, all right. Just don't eat my head.'

The grease would be combined with mud, slime and permanent purple dye. The concoction would be reserved for the lowliest enemies. Elderly relatives got a sampling of the more dignified, store-bought powders, yellow, red and green. For our best friends, we prepared a golden paint, carefully mixing real gilt and oil in a small jar.

Madhur Jaffrey

RAMADAN AND EID-UL-FITR

Ramadan is the name of the month in the Muslim calendar prior to the festival of Eid-Ul-Fitr. It is a month of fasting for most Muslim people who do not eat or drink between the times of sunrise and sunset, a time when they are reminded of the importance of God.

Ramadan and Eid-Ul-Fitr may fall on any month of the Gregorian calendar. This is because Muslims follow the lunar calendar. A new moon appears every 29 or 30 days so the lunar calendar is 11 days shorter than the Gregorian calendar which normally has 365 days. Thus, the length of the day's fasting differs from year to year depending on the times of sunrise and sunset.

According to the Qur'an every Muslim must give a sum of money to charity. At the end of Ramadan, on the day of Eid-Ul-Fitr the contribution is known as Zakat-Ul-Fitr. 'Zakat' means an offering given for the poor. The amount is decided by the community.

During the month of Ramadan, too, Muslims celebrate one of the most important events in their history; this is called the Night of Power and is the time when the Prophet Muhammad began to receive the Holy Qur'an from Allah. Many Muslims try to recite the whole of the Qur'an during Ramadan. They also remember some of the important events in the life of Muhammad and make a special effort to behave in ways which will make them better Muslims.

The end of Ramadan is a very exciting time in Muslim homes. Everyone waits for the appearance of the new moon, the first glimpse of which marks the end of fast and brings joy as the celebrations of Eid-Ul-Fitr begin. Eid-Ul-Fitr is a family celebration. After bathing, people wear their finest, often new, clothes and share a meal together. Families will then visit the mosque where special prayers are offered and Zakat is given. On returning home presents may be exchanged and sweets such as sheer khorma are eaten. There is a special meal for which family and friends may get together and the greeting 'Eid Mubarak' is frequently exchanged. These words are often found on the cards traditionally sent at Eid.

In addition to the feasting and celebrating, Eid is also a day to remember and pray for members of the family who have died.

A long time to go

It was Ramadan, the month of the Fast. Every day Rahilla asked her mother, 'Is it Eid yet, Mummy? Is it Eid today?'

Every day her mother said, 'Not yet, Rahilla. When the New Moon is seen in the sky, then it will be Eid.'

Eid-el-Fitr is the big celebration that Muslims have at the end of the Fast. There are presents and lovely food to eat. Everyone goes to the Mosque to meet and pray together. Relations come to the house and the children all get new clothes and gifts of money. It is like some other people's Christmas Day.

Every evening when it grew dark, Rahilla would gaze out of the window at the sky, looking for the new moon.

Her mother said, 'You can't see it from this country, Rahilla. When they see the New Moon in Arabia, they will telephone to the big Mosque in London, and the people in the big Mosque will telephone to all the other Mosques in the country and they will tell us when it is Eid.'

Rahilla did not like the month of the Fast. Every night after she had gone to sleep, she would be woken up by her mother and father and the big children getting up. They would wash and dress and say their prayers, then they would sit down to a big meal at two o'clock in the morning. They would talk and eat and be together.

Rahilla would lie in bed, listening to the talk. She could smell the delicious smell of the food drifting up from downstairs and, although she was too sleepy to want any, she did not like to be left out. Sometimes she would creep out of bed and down the stairs to where the family was eating and sometimes her mother would let her stay and have something, and at other times she would be cross and send her back to bed. The meal that the family ate then was all that they would have until nine o'clock the next evening. It was a long time to go.

Rahilla was the youngest in the family. All her brothers and sisters were allowed to fast like their parents.

'I want to fast. I want to fast,' said Rahilla

'You're too little,' said her mother. 'Wait until you're as big as Ali, then you can fast like the rest of us.'

'No! I want to fast *now*! I want to fast *now*!' said Rahilla.

Then her mother got cross. She said, 'You're too little. Now don't let me hear any more about it.'

'Why do people fast then?' asked Rahilla.

'Because God has told us to. And also it helps us to remember all those people who never have enough to eat,' said her mother. 'People who are always hungry, and who sometimes die because they are so hungry.'

In spite of what her mother had said, Rahilla decided that she was going to fast. She thought, I shall fast for a whole day, and then Mummy will see that I am as big as the others.

Rahilla's parents were always asleep in bed when she left for school. They were tired after being awake so long at night. Often, long after the meal had been cleared away and the children had gone back to bed, they would stay awake to pray and read the Koran.

Her big sister used to give her something to eat – cornflakes or bread and jam. This morning, Rahilla hid the bread and jam under a chair before she left.

In school, at milk time, when the milk monitors were giving out the bottles, Rahilla said, 'I don't want any today – and no biscuits either.'

'Why don't you want your milk?' asked her teacher, Mrs Davis. 'Your mother has paid for it, you know – and for the biscuits. She wants you to have them every day.'

'I don't want any,' said Rahilla, and shut her lips tightly.

Mrs Davis put the milk and biscuits down in front of Rahilla and said, 'Come along now – try and have them, there's a good girl!'

Rahilla wanted to drink that milk. She wanted, more than anything, to eat the biscuits. But she knew that she had decided to fast, so she said, 'I don't want it thank you,' and she left them there until it was playtime, and Mrs Davis said, 'Oh well, if you won't have it, you won't. But I shall send a note to your mother to let her know.'

When it was dinner time, Rahilla tried to stay out in the playground, but the dinner lady collected up all the children, and when Rahilla said, 'I don't want dinner today,' the dinner lady said, 'Nonsense! Go and wash your hands and get into line.'

Rahilla went into the dinner hall. She took a tray and went to the counter where the cooks were serving out the dinners. They gave her fish fingers, potato and carrots, and there was sponge pudding and custard. Rahilla felt so hungry she thought she would start to cry. She took her tray to the table and she said, 'I don't want any, thank you.'

The dinner ladies came up to her. They tried to make her eat. They put some fish and potato on a fork and held it by her mouth saying, 'Come on, lovey – just try it.' But Rahilla would not open her mouth. They fetched Mrs Davis, who said, 'She didn't have any milk either today. I think the child must be ill.' And she felt Rahilla's forehead and sent her to lie down in a special little room where sick children went.

When it was time for afternoon school, Mrs Davis came and asked Rahilla if she would like to go home.

'No thank you,' said Rahilla, 'I'd like to go back to the classroom.'

That afternoon was Hobby Afternoon. The children were allowed to choose what they would like to do. Some of the children went with the lady who helped Mrs Davis to make cakes in the school kitchen. They made fairy cakes with pink icing on top, and there were thirty six of them – one for each child and one for the teachers. 'I don't want one, thank you,' Rahilla said, very near to tears. She could hardly stop herself from snatching up the little cake and stuffing it into her mouth.

'Oh come along – do eat one, Rahilla,' said Mrs Davis.

Rahilla took a cake and gave it to Manjit who sat next to her, 'Would you like it, Manjit?' she said.

'Oh yes please!' said Manjit. She ate the two cakes very quickly.

When Rahilla got home, her mother was in the bedroom sewing. Rahilla went to watch the television. Her tummy was really hurting. She knew that her mother did not start to prepare the evening meal until eight o'clock, when it was dark, and she herself was getting ready for bed. She waited and waited until at last her mother and grandmother went into the kitchen to start the cooking. Rahilla began to smell the rich smells of curry and spices. She could hear her grandmother rolling and slapping the *chapattis*. She held her tummy and rocked about. I don't like fasting, she thought, I'm glad I don't have to do it every day.

When the meal was ready, Rahilla rushed into the kitchen to fetch her plate. Her mother gave her some rice and curry and *chapattis*.

'Can I have more?' asked Rahilla.

Her mother was surprised but she put some more on the plate. Rahilla sat down on the floor and ate it all up in just a few minutes.

'Why, Rahilla!' said her mother. 'You look as if you haven't eaten for a week!' Rahilla hid her face in her hands.

'Have you had anything to eat today?' said her mother. Rahilla shook her head. She went to her coat and fetched the note from Mrs Davis.

'Why didn't you eat your dinner – and your milk and biscuits?' asked her mother when she had read it. 'Are you sick?'

'I wanted to remember the little children who don't have enough to eat. I wanted to fast like the others,' said Rahilla.

Her mother smiled. 'Well, now you know what it feels like, do you still want to fast?'

'No,' said Rahilla, munching a *chapatti*, 'I don't like it at all. I think I'll wait till I'm bigger.'

Nadya Smith

Eid-Ul-Fitr

Like a sliver of lemon
In the evening sky
The new moon rises,
Ramadan has past,
The fasting is done,
Tomorrow is the feast
Of Eid-Ul-Fitr,
We will eat spicy meat
And delicious samosas,
I will greet my neighbours,
My friends on the street,
May the peace of God
And the blessing of Eid
Be with you.

Theresa Heine

This is our Eid (Hamaree Eid)

Traditional Urdu

Starting note: D

Chorus

Ha - ma - ree Ei - d, hay jee Eid, Ha -

ma - ree Ei - d, hay jee Eid, Ha - ma - ree Ei - d, hay jee Eid, Ha -

Fine

ma - ree Ei - d, hay jee Eid. 1. Arr, Ham ne na - maz par - hee,

(After repeat, spoken:) "Purr aaj" *(Repeat chorus)*

aur roz - ey bhee___ ra - khey.___ 2. Arr, Ham ne la - doo kh'a - ee,___

(After repeat, spoken:) "Kyoon kay aaj" *(Repeat chorus)*

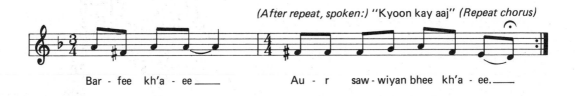

Bar - fee kh'a - ee___ Au - r saw - wiyan bhee kh'a - ee.___

3. Arr, Ham ne n - 'ay kap - prey sil - w'ae,___

(After repeat, spoken:) "Kyoon kay aaj" *(Repeat chorus)*

Aur choo - ri - an bhee___ peh - neen.___ 4. Arr,

(After repeat, spoken:) "Kyoon kay aaj" *(Repeat chorus)*

Ham ne mahn-dee la - g'a - ee___ Au - r khush -ian ma - n'a - ee.___

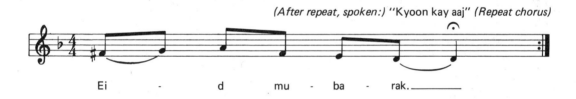

5. Arr, Sab - ko Eid mu - ba - rak,___ Eid mu - ba - rak,___

(After repeat, spoken:) "Kyoon kay aaj" *(Repeat chorus)*

Ei - d mu - ba - rak._____

This is our Eid festival!

We have said our prayers
and we fasted,
But now it is our Eid festival.

We eat our ladoo, our barfee
and sawwiyan
Because now it is our Eid festival.

We wear our new clothes
and our bangles
Because now...

We have enjoyed decorating
our hands with mahndee
Because now...

Greetings and congratulations to
all on our Eid festival.

Festival of fast-breaking

The peace of God be with you –
'Id Mubarak,' we say,
'Asalama Alaykum'
on this especial day.
We wear our finest dresses
and wash and comb our hair,
and lay and spread the table –
Let's all share!

A generous gift will feed him
who stands beside the door -
how shall he join the feasting
if he be plain and poor?
So let us sit, rejoicing
on this most holy day
and welcome in our neighbour.
'Id Mubarak!' we say.

Jean Kenward

PASSOVER

The Jewish festival of Passover takes place on 14th–21st of the Jewish month of Nisan (March or April). The Jewish name for the festival is Pesach. In biblical times Passover was kept for seven days and the festival now lasts for eight days. Orthodox Jews will not work on the first or last two days of Passover.

The annual celebration of Passover is a commemoration of the time when the Jewish people were slaves of the Egyptians, and Moses led them across the Red Sea to safety and freedom in the Promised Land.

In Jewish homes there is much preparation before the Passover celebration. All foods containing leaven (yeast) are taken from the house which is cleaned from top to bottom, especially the kitchen. Many families keep special sets of crockery and cutlery for use during Passover, so these are brought out and the everyday ones put away.

Each year in many families just before Passover celebrations start, the children are given a candle and feather and are told to hunt for any remaining leaven or chametz (the father will have hidden several pieces) and when everyone is certain none is left in the house, the celebration can truly begin.

When the family gathers for the Passover meal or Seder, the youngest member of the family asks questions about the origin and meaning of the feast and these are answered in a traditional form by the head of the household. The symbolism of the special items on the table is explained, thus retelling the story of the first Passover. This story of Passover is told in the Haggadah, the book used for the Seder. The meal begins with a blessing and the lighting of two candles.

On the Seder table there will be three pieces of matzah and a Seder plate with special foods: a bone, a roasted egg, parsley, bitter herbs and charoset. The bone (called z'roah) represents the Passover lamb eaten long ago by the Jews to remember that God passed over the homes of the Jewish slaves in Egypt and spared them from the punishments given to the Egyptians. The bitter herbs, known as maror, are eaten as a reminder of the bitter lives the Jewish people in Egypt were forced to live as slaves of the Egyptians. They had to work very hard building cities, and the brown charoset (made from cinnamon, apples and wine) represents the clay used for the bricks. The bitter herbs and charoset are eaten together.

The matzah is eaten as a reminder of when the Jews were told to leave Egypt immediately and were unable to bake proper bread as the yeast in the dough would not have had time to rise. Instead they baked thin leaves of unleavened bread called matzah or matzot. The parsley (karpas) is a symbol of new life. It is dipped in saltwater before it is eaten; this saltwater is a reminder of the tears shed by the Jewish slaves in Egypt when they begged God to save them from their suffering. The suffering of the Egyptians is also remembered in the symbolic spilling of one drop of wine for each of the ten plagues God sent. Also on the table will be extra cup of wine; this is known as Elijah's cup.

It's Passover time

Linda Tsuruoka

Set the ta - ble pour out the wine, Se - der's here it's
Pass - o - ver time. Tell the an - cient sto - ry once more,
That is what the Se - der is for. Set a place for E - li - ya - hu,
Ask four ques - tions sing Da - ye - nu, Hide the mat - za
dip in the wine, Se - der's here it's Pass - o - ver time.

Different from other nights

As we were getting ready to go to my Aunt Ruth's house, my dad said, 'Your brother likes the Passover because he thinks he's the star of the show. He's asked the Four Questions for the last couple of years and no one dares to let him know this is his last time as the youngest child in the family who can speak properly. Next year, your cousin Becky will be four, and she's a big talker already. She'll ask the questions.'

I nodded. I'd been the youngest once and it was exciting, standing up in front of the whole family, looking down the yards and yards of white tablecloth and asking the questions that were part of the Passover service. I still remember them. They all wanted to know the same thing: Why is this night different from other nights? Why on this night do we eat unleavened bread and bitter herbs? Why do we sit on cushions? Why do we do things in an unusual way? And the answers, when they came, helped to unfold the story of the Passover before the banquet began.

When it was my turn, I'd spent days and days practising the words in Hebrew. My parents had listened to me until, as my mother put it, 'I heard questions every night in my dreams' and still I'd stumbled and stuttered a bit over the strange sounds when all those smiling faces were turned to look at me.

I was delighted when Danny took over the main part in the Seder night drama. He is only six and a half and this is the third year he's done it.

'Seder night suits your Aunt Ruth as well,' Dad said as we set out in the car. 'Did you know that the word 'seder' means 'order'? If anyone approves of order, it's my big sister.'

That was quite true. Our Aunt Ruth is the tidiest, cleanest, most orderly person I've ever seen. At Passover time, when the whole house has to be cleaned from top to bottom so that not one crumb is left lurking in any hidden corner, Aunt Ruth goes through the rooms like a tornado, dusters flying, Hoover purring, wet cloths at the ready. It would be a brave crumb that dared to stay in her house. She enjoyed cleaning so much that Danny and I never offered to help her, but we both liked getting the special foods ready, so Dad always took us over early in the afternoon, and Aunt Ruth always greeted us with the same cry, 'It's my assistants! Welcome! I've kept all the exciting things for you to do.'

Danny wasn't old enough to do any chopping, so what he was allowed to do was mainly mixing. He didn't really care. He only came for the story. Every year he'd heard it, here in the kitchen, and every year he'd listened to it during the Seder meal, and still he wanted it once more. I didn't say anything, because I liked it as well. It was one of the most exciting stories I knew, and enjoyed the way Aunt Ruth told it, as if it had happened yesterday instead of thousands of years ago, as if she personally knew somebody who had been a slave in Egypt.

'Tell us the story,' Danny said, mashing at the apples I was giving him as I peeled them. He was making a terrible mess but even Aunt Ruth didn't mind. She took a deep breath.

'Once upon a time,' she began (because to her, a story wasn't a story unless it started like that) 'the Israelites were slaves in Egypt. They were used as labour to build pyramids, dragging the bricks everywhere in that terrible heat, can you imagine? Danny, try and keep the apples in the dish. What you're mashing up there is apples for the haroset. We put cinnamon and nuts in it, and a bit of red wine, and we eat it in memory of the slaves.

It looks like the mortar they used to spread on the bricks, to stick them together.'

Danny looked at his squashed apples and began to mash them a little more energetically.

'Now the leader of the Jews,' said Aunt Ruth 'was called Moses...'

'...like Grandpa Moses, said Danny.

'Yes, like Grandpa... this other Moses went to Pharaoh, who was the king of Egypt, and asked him to stop treating the Jews as slaves, to let them be free, and of course you can imagine what Pharaoh said.'

'He said no!' Danny was jumping up and down because we were getting to the best bit of the story. 'And then Moses told God and God got angry and he sent the ten plagues!'

'Do you remember them?' Aunt Ruth said and she ticked them off on her fingers. 'Blood, frogs, lice, beasts, blight, boils, hail, locusts, darkness and slaying of the first born.' She shivered. 'Can you imagine how dreadful they must have been? All the poor Egyptians with itchy scalps, in the dark, hail falling all over the place, full of painful boils, who knows where on their bodies, and treading on frogs every time they put their foot on the ground? Not to mention rivers running with blood and no crops to make food with because of blight and locusts? Terrible, really terrible. And most of all, can you picture all those poor children dying?' Aunt Ruth shook her head. 'The Angel of Death knew which were the Jewish houses because Moses had told all the Jews to smear the door posts and lintels of their houses with the blood of a lamb, so that the Angel could pass over those houses and spare the people living in them...'

'...and that's why it's called The Passover!' Danny finished in triumph.

'Exactly. Now put these chopped nuts into the apple and keep mixing. After all those plagues the Pharaoh couldn't wait to get rid of the Jews, so off they went, and they spent forty years in the desert and eventually came to the Promised Land, the land of milk and honey, and here's a bit of honey to put into the haroset because I'm not sure the apples are sweet enough.'

Danny stirred the honey round into the pinkish-grey mixture in front of him. I thought about the plagues. I'm ten now, but when I was Danny's age, I was terrified of them. Grandpa Moses had a very old book in which the order of the Passover service was printed. This book was called the Haggadah, and in it there were pictures illustrating the ten plagues. I hated those pictures. They were tiny but horrifying: a woman dipping her hand in a waterfall of blood, frogs jumping out of somebody's bed, boils all over a young man's face, and worst of all, the wide, black wings of the Angel of Death taking up almost the whole of one picture. I told my mother how frightened I was and she said, 'You shouldn't look at them.'

'I know,' I'd answered, 'but it's funny. I can't *not* look at them. I don't want to see them and yet I do.' Danny isn't a bit scared, but then he's always been quite bloodthirsty.

There was another scary bit of the story. I reminded Aunt Ruth about it. 'You left out the part about the Red Sea,' I said.

Aunt Ruth smiled. 'I'm sorry. I'm thinking about my matzo balls... well, the Egyptians were chasing the Israelites and when they got to the Red Sea, it looked as though they would be caught and killed by Pharaoh's soldiers, but God made a miracle, and the waves rolled back and all the Israelites walked along a nice dry path to the other bank through a kind of tunnel where the walls were made of water piled up, like towering blue mountains. When the Egyptians made the mistake of following them, the water suddenly decided to roll back to its usual place, and so, of course, the soldiers were all drowned. Aunt Ruth wiped her floury hands on her apron.

'Now, go and play, both of you, and in a little while you can help me lay the table.'

The table had to be laid in a very special way. There were always the Passover dishes and knives and forks, which were only used for one week in the year, and there was the beautiful white tablecloth with lace around the edges and white embroidery in the corners. It was enormous, bigger than any tablecloth I'd ever seen. The two dishes in front of Grandpa's place at the table had on them all the things that were needed for the ceremony. One plate had on it bitter herbs called maror, which was really grated horseradish, and which was eaten in memory of the bitterness of slavery and also the haroset representing mortar, a hard-boiled egg (because Passover was a spring festival), a roasted lamb-bone, a piece of celery and some salt water to dip it into. The other plate had on it three slices of matzo. Matzos are like big square crackers, and we ate them, I knew, because when the Israelites fled, they didn't have time to bake proper bread with yeast. That's one of the best bits of the Seder. The children are allowed to hide a piece of matzo called the Afikoman and we only tell the grown-ups where it is when they give us chocolates at the end of the meal. Last year, Danny got into trouble because it was his idea to hide the Afikoman in the video machine, but this year it's my turn to choose a place, and I've thought of a good spot... in Aunt Ruth's apron pocket. She'll have hung it behind the kitchen door and no one will think of looking there.

Danny had disappeared into Aunt Ruth's spare bedroom to play with the toys she kept for any visiting nieces and nephews. There was a box of toy cars, some plastic animals, lots of books and a bag full of wooden bricks. Aunt Ruth and I finished laying the table without his help.

'Don't forget to put out an extra chair for Elijah the Prophet,' said Aunt Ruth.

'I used to be scared of Elijah,' I said. 'When I was little. I couldn't understand why he'd never come even though we called and called him.'

Aunt Ruth laughed. 'Didn't you know Elijah was from the Bible?'

'No,' I said. 'I thought he was a relative. That was bad enough, but when I realised he'd been dead for hundreds of years, it was even worse. I started expecting a ghost.'

'It's just a tradition, that's all,' said Aunt Ruth. 'Some people believe the empty chair is really in case an unexpected guest should appear... which reminds me... they'll all be here soon. We should go and get ready.'

There were twenty people round the table for the Seder meal, and every one of them was dressed up as if for a party. Even Cousin Becky sat round-eyed and silent for once, as though she were learning everything thoroughly so as to be ready when her turn came next year. Danny's face and hands were shining with cleanliness, I knew, because I'd been put in charge of getting him ready. It had been hard work because he never stood still even for one second, but he looked as good as gold now and I felt quite proud of him.

Grandpa Moses came in carrying the Haggadah with the pictures of the plagues in it. He looked more and more like the Biblical Moses every year, with his thick snow-white eyebrows and beard. The whole family fell silent as he sat down. He peered at the two dishes in front of him and then looked up and said, 'Ruth?'

'Yes, Father.'

'Why is there an empty dish where the haroset should be?'

'Nonsense, Father, of course the haroset's there. I put it there myself. Naomi will tell you.' She turned to me.

'Yes, Grandpa,' I nodded. 'It was there. I saw Aunt Ruth putting it there. Danny and I helped her to make it.' My voice faded to nothing.

'Well,' said Grandpa Moses. 'Perhaps someone has eaten it? Maybe it was so delicious, the children couldn't resist... children? Have you been dipping fingers into the dish? Do not be afraid to tell me.'

All of us, me and my cousins and Danny too, shook our heads and said no.

'Well,' Grandpa Moses sat back in his chair. 'This is a mystery. I do not like mysteries, therefore I shall sit here. We shall sit here until someone tells me what has happened to the haroset.'

I don't know how long Grandpa Moses would really have waited, but Danny I know couldn't bear the thought of not asking the questions, of not hearing the story or eating all Aunt Ruth's lovely food and of not

finding the Afikoman. He said, 'Grandpa, I took the haroset. I'm sorry. I didn't think it was so important.'

Grandpa Moses looked through his spectacles at Danny. 'Really? Did you eat it? Could you not wait for the rest of us?'

'I didn't eat it,' said Danny. 'I used it to make a pyramid.'

'Make a pyramid? Where? Why? From what?'

'From bricks. In Aunt Ruth's spare bedroom. On the floor. I used haroset to stick the bricks together. It worked, as well. Aunt Ruth said it was like mortar. I was being an Israelite.'

'I see,' said Grandpa Moses, trying hard not to laugh. 'In that case, I don't feel I can punish you. You were simply re-enacting the story of our ancestors.'

Aunt Ruth jumped out of her chair.

'I shall make some more... it'll only take a second. Everything is ready in the kitchen; all the nuts are ground up already.'

Eventually, the Seder began. Cousin Becky had fallen asleep with her head on the white tablecloth. After the four questions were over, after all the readings and the prayers and the songs were finished, after the door had been opened to let Elijah in, Grandpa Moses turned to Danny.

'You asked before: how is this night different from all other nights, and I will tell you the answer. Of the eighty Seder nights that I can remember in my lifetime, *this* is the only one where the haroset was used to build a real pyramid. I shall remember it....'

I'll remember it too. I was the one who had to help Danny wash and dry every single one of Aunt Ruth's bricks.

Adèle Geras

The ballad of the four sons

The following song to the tune of 'Clementine' is not included in the real Haggadah. However, the questions of each of the four sons and answers to them found in this song are based on those given in the Haggadah.

Said the father to his children:
'At the Seder you will dine,
You will eat your fill the matzah,
You will drink four cups of wine.'

Now this father had no daughters,
But his sons they numbered four,
One was wise and one was wicked,
One was simple and a bore.

And the fourth was sweet and winsome,
He was young and he was small
While his brothers asked the questions,
He could hardly speak at all.

WHAT DOES THE WISE SON SAY?

Said the wise son to his father,
'Would you please explain the laws?
All the customs of the Seder
Will you please explain their cause?'

And the father proudly answered,
'As our fathers ate in speed,
Ate the paschal lamb 'ere midnight
And from the slavery they were freed.

So we all follow their example
And 'ere midnight must complete
The service of the Seder;
After twelve we may not eat.'

AND WHAT DOES THE WICKED SON SAY?

Then did sneer the son so wicked,
'What does all this mean to you?'
And the father's voice was bitter
As his grief and anger grew.

'If yourself you don't consider
A true son of Israel,
Then for you this has no meaning,
You could be a slave as well.'

AND THE SIMPLE SON, WHAT DOES HE SAY?

Then the simple son said simply,
'What is this?' and then quietly,
The good father told his offspring,
'We were freed from slavery.'

AND THE SON WHO DOES NOT YET KNOW HOW TO ASK?

But the youngest son was silent,
For he could not ask at all,
His eyes were bright with wonder,
As his father told them all.

Now dear children, heed the lesson,
And remember evermore,
What the father told the children,
Told his sons that numbered four.

Anonymous

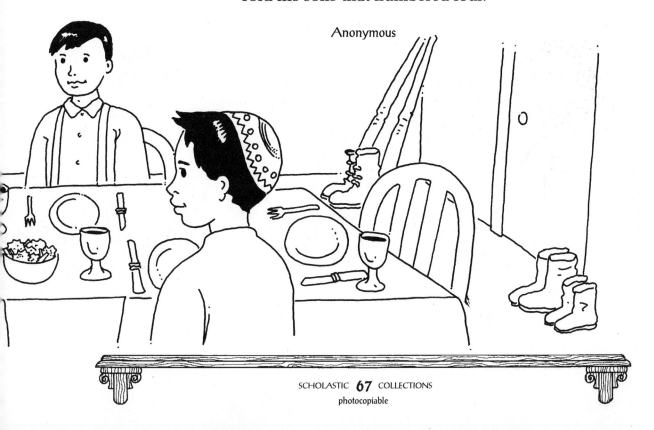

Seder

Why celebrate with bitter herbs,
salt tears of still-remembered slaves
and (though there's time now
for less hasty ways) this joyless bread?

The salt reminds us still
of parting seas,
and, though there's time now,
once was none;
whilst plague took
Egypt's eldest sons
we brought to safety
our firstborn.

Pass over, Death;
Pass over, Death;
Passover....

Judith Nicholls

The Passover story

'Now you're to be freed from the Egyptians,' God said,
'You must not wait to bake your bread,'
Then God passed over the homes of each Jew,
But Egyptian's first born males he slew.

The shops each year our Matzos supplies,
The bread of slavery that does not rise,
A shin bone of lamb we put aside,
For the Paschal lamb in the temple died.

Bitter herbs on the table we lay,
For embittered slaves of former days,
Forced by their masters to make bricks in the sun,
From Egyptian whips they could not run.

When it's a Passover meal we must all be there,
To eat special food, that our mothers prepare,
Food that reminds us of the freed Israelites,
As we read the Haggadah by candle light.

Janet E. Greenyer

EASTER

The word Easter comes from Eostre, the name of the goddess of spring who, in pre-Christian times in North Europe, was honoured annually at the time of the spring equinox, a time of new life.

For Christian people Easter is the most important festival of the year. Christians believe that Jesus is the son of God and that after being crucified he rose from the dead and it is his resurrection, a victory over death, which they remember and celebrate on Easter Sunday. In Western churches Easter Day falls on the first Sunday after the spring full moon, either March or April; in Eastern churches it may fall up to five weeks later, in April or May.

The Sunday before Easter Sunday is known as Palm Sunday and commemorates Jesus' entry into Jerusalem. On this day palm crosses are given out in churches in memory of the palm leaves waved to welcome Jesus as he rode into Jerusalem. The week from Palm Sunday to Easter Sunday is known a Holy Week during which Christians pray and think about the events that took place in Jesus' life during that time. On Maundy Thursday the last communion supper which Jesus and his disciples shared is celebrated; Good Friday, which commemorates Jesus' Crucifixion on the hill of Calvary, is a day of prayer on which many Christians participate in a three-hour service starting at 3pm, the time of Jesus' death.

Next comes Easter Sunday, a time of rejoicing, a time for giving thanks for that first Easter Sunday morning when some of Jesus' disciples went to the tomb where his body had been laid; Mary Magdalen and then Simon Peter discovered that the body had gone and were told by angels that Jesus had risen. On Easter Sunday churches are full of flowers, and Easter eggs are given to children as symbols of new life. Eggs have always been a symbol of fertility and new life and Easter eggs, either hard-boiled and decorated on the shell in paint, wax or dyes, or made of chocolate, form an important part of traditional Easter celebrations.

The eating of hot-cross buns, now a Good Friday tradition, also dates back to pre-Christian celebrations in Roman times when small wheat cakes or buns were made. These were divided into four by a cross which stood for the four phases of the moon. The cross on Good Friday hot-cross buns now symbolises the cross on Calvary.

The symbols of Easter

David Moses

1. The dark-ness drove the light from the sky On the day our Lord was cru-ci-fied, And___ those who sealed him___ in his grave Did-n't know their Lord would rise a-gain. *Chorus* But on that ve-ry first Eas-ter Day, When they saw the stone was

rolled a - way And the bat -tle to con - quer Death was won, Then his

fol-low-ers knew Life___ had just be - gun. (Now...)

2. Now, Easter's a time for lots of fun,
With chocolate eggs and hot cross buns,
While nature glows with a life that's new.
The rain clouds part and the sun shines through.

Chorus

3. Those Easter buns which taste so nice
Still hot from the oven, with a scent of spice,
Light brown on the top with a white sugar cross
To recall how Jesus died for us.

Chorus

4. You can boil an egg or colour its shell,
Buy an egg made out of chocolate as well.
But the egg broken open at Easter tide
Is an empty tomb and a brand new life.

Last chorus:
And on this very next Easter Day
Remember a stone was rolled away.
Now the battle to conquer Death is won,
There's a chance of a new life
For everyone.

New life

Gill Wilson

1. Lit - tle fluf - fy bun - nies, ___ Wool - ly lamb - kins too.

Yel - low East - er chick - ens, ___ All from God to you.

Chorus

East - er's here, let's clap our hands, Clap our hands for joy. God

gave his Son at East - er time. Clap our hands for joy.

2. New life in the hedgerows,
In the garden too.
New life in the farmyard,
All from God to you.

Chorus

Easter

It was the last day of the Easter term – and it was one of those mornings when everything goes wrong. Betsy had been playing with the alarm clock the day before and had switched off the alarm, so Mum woke up later than usual. She was in the kitchen now, still in her dressing gown, making toast for Foxy. Betsy was sitting in her high chair, feeding herself mushy cereal – that is, when her spoon found her mouth; sometimes it found her nose or her hair.

'She ought to wear a fisherman's cape for meals,' said Foxy. 'Then you could just hose her down afterwards.'

Gran came in looking early morning-ish and screwing up her eyes.

'Anyone feen my teef?' she asked. 'And where'f my glaffef? I need fem to find my teef.'

She felt her way to the kitchen table and trod on Smokey's tail. Smokey squealed and squeezed under the cooker. Foxy's Dad came into the kitchen, which was only small even when it was empty.

'A cup of tea going, is there?' he asked.

Mum turned to put tea bags and boiling water into the teapot. Gran bent down to get Smokey out.

'Come on, come on out, good puss,' she coaxed.

'The toast, Mum, quick,' said Foxy. 'It's burning.'

'Burning, burning – 'ray, 'ray!' cried Betsy. She waved her spoon enthusiastically and a glob of cereal flew across and landed on Smokey, who hissed and shot back under the cooker.

'Now look what you've done,' said Gran.

She straightened up and banged her head on the grill pan, which Mum had just pulled out to blow

out the flames on the toast.

'Here's your glasses, Gran,' said Dad.

'Where? Where?' said Gran, rubbing her head with one hand and holding out the other one for the glasses. Dad reached across to give her them and trod in Smokey's saucer of milk. Mum threw the burnt toast in the bin and laid some more slices on the grill pan. Dad hopped round on one foot looking for something to wipe off the milk with. As he did so, another of Betsy's cereal globs landed on his clean foot. It was at this moment that Foxy suddenly remembered.

'Oh, Mum, I've got to take a hard-boiled egg – I've *got* to.'

There was a moment's silence, as all heads turned to look at him.

'A hard boiled egg?' said his mother, faintly. '– Now?'

'It's for a competition,' said Foxy. 'We're going to decorate them for an Easter egg competition.'

'Choccy, choccy, choccy!' shouted Betsy; she knew about Easter eggs.

Dad found a duster and wiped his feet with it.

'Here we are,' said Mum, ferreting about at the back of the fridge. 'It's the last one in the box; it's got a big crack in it.'

'The toast, Mum, it's burning,' cried Foxy again.

''Ray, 'ray!' shouted Betsy excitedly; breakfast wasn't usually this much fun. She raked through her hair with her slimy spoon. Mum blew out more flames.

'This teapot always dribbles,' grumbled Dad, pouring out tea into the mugs and over the table.

Gran picked up the duster to polish her glasses.

'That'f funny, they're all fmeary.' She screwed up her eyes again and wandered out to look for her teeth. Mum put the egg into boiling water in a saucepan. The water immediately foamed with strings of floating egg white.

'I don't think I'm hungry after all,' said Foxy, as his mother lobbed the second lot of black toast into the bin. He finished off the tea in his mug and started to get his things ready for school.

'Where's my felt-tips, Mum?' he asked.

'Gran had them,' she said. 'She was doing some sort of a competition for Blue Peter with Betsy – where did you put those felt-tips, Betsy?'

'Underpsshed,' said Betsy through a mouthful.

'Oh, no,' groaned Foxy – that meant she'd pushed them into her secret place under the shed and he'd have to grovel in the wet grass trying to reach them.

'I'll have to go without them. Is the egg ready, Mum?'

His mother stared at him.

'The egg? – Oops, the egg!'

She dived for the pan which was hissing and spluttering as it boiled dry.

'Well, it's certainly *hard*-boiled,' she said, peering into the brownish pan. She spooned out the cracked, discoloured egg, dropped it into a paper bag and gave it to Foxy.

'Bye, everybody,' he shouted, and hurried off to school.

Not surprisingly, Foxy's egg decoration wasn't very successful. For a start, he hadn't his own felt-tips, so he had to keep begging to borrow other people's. They wanted to use their brightest colours, so he only managed to get brown, black and a sort of sludgy green.

'You could pretend it was a camouflaged egg,' suggested Imran, 'Like they have in the army.'

'Why do they want camouflaged eggs in the army?' asked Foxy.

'Well, so the enemy can't see them, I suppose,' said Imran.

Foxy decided against that idea. He set to work to turn his egg into a tortoise. The cracks helped to make the pattern of its shell look quite realistic. He drew its head and four feet and a tiny tail.

'That's really good,' said Imran. 'Really.'

But Foxy knew that Imran's Spiderman egg was much better – and so were several of the others, decorated in clear, bright colours. The Headmaster came in later to judge the eggs. He gave first prize to a really clever face that one of the girls had drawn, second prize to Imran's Spiderman, and third prize to an egg covered in brilliant little butterflies. 'That's great, Immy!' said Foxy, clapping his friend on the back. Everyone except the three winners was secretly disappointed, although Foxy had been pretty sure he wouldn't win; his rather messy design looked more like a stone than a tortoise. The Headmaster stopped on his way out.

'Now don't forget, everyone,' he said. 'Come to the Hall after dinner, for our grand Class Egg Rolling Competition.'

Foxy had forgotten the egg-rolling; it was quite a tradition. Usually the PE benches were lined up, end to end, and rubber mats were placed over them, hanging down to the floor. They provided a slope down which the eggs were rolled. A class at a time knelt behind the benches and let go of their eggs to see which one rolled furthest down the mats and away across the floor of the Hall.

This time four classes went through their heats, and four children excitedly clutched their winning eggs. Then came the turn of Foxy's class. He and Imran and the others knelt down behind the PE benches. They each held their egg on the very edge of the bench, so that it had a good long slope to roll down to give it the best start.

'Go!' ordered the Headmaster.

Eggs of all colours hurtled down the slope and sped across the mats. Some trundled to a stop, some went this way and that, bumping into others. A bright one shot across the floor, followed more slowly by Foxy's tortoise. But then the red one suddenly spun round and came back the way it had gone, leaving the tortoise rolling on until it came to a hesitant stop, furthest from the bench.

'You've won this round!' said Imran, slapping Foxy on the back in his turn.

Foxy grinned and went to collect his prize, a cream egg. He and Imran shared it, a bite at a time, while they waited for the final play-off between all the winning eggs. Foxy found himself right in the middle of the row of competitors. He was afraid that might not be a favourable position, as the other eggs would probably roll into the middle and stop the tortoise short. He held his egg on the extreme edge of the bench, determined at least to start the race well.

'Go!' said the Headmaster.

The eggs hurtled down the slope. A Humpty-Dumpty shot ahead, doing fast roly-polies across the floor. A striped egg went sideways, cracking into two others, so that all three came to a stop. A bright blue one seemed to be made of rubber, it was almost bouncing along. The audience was laughing and cheering the eggs on. The tortoise was slowly crawling across the floor behind the rest.

'Oh, go on, go on,' urged Foxy. 'Go *on*, tortoise!'

'Come-on-*tor*-toise,' chanted Foxy's class. 'Come-on-*tor*-toise.'

The Humpty-Dumpty and most of the others had wandered to the sides of the Hall; the tortoise was at least still moving forward, but slowing down.

'Come-on-*tor*-toise,' chanted Mr Tucker's class, louder than ever.

The bouncing blue egg suddenly twizzled round and lurched into the tortoise, sending it forward. Then the blue bouncer stopped. But the tortoise was still lumbering on. They all held their breath until it eventually came to a halt only a metre from the Headmaster's feet.

'The tortoise is the winner!' he declared, laughing and holding it up on high. Rousing cheers from Mr Tucker's class filled the Hall.

'You've done it, you've done it again,' shouted Imran, pushing him forward. Foxy couldn't believe his luck as the Headmaster shook his hand and gave him back the tortoise egg and a prize. There were more cheers as Foxy grinned and went back to his classmates. He couldn't wait to get home and tell everyone his good news.

'Hello, Foxy,' said Gran, who had found her teeth. 'Goodness, look at your hands – "What, will these hands ne'er be clean?" – they're covered in paint.'

'No, Gran that's felt-tip,' he said. 'It got on there when I was decorating my egg for the competition.'

Betsy came toddling over to have a look. Then Foxy told them all about the egg-decorating competition and the tortoise, and how it had managed to win his class heat, and then the Grand Final of the egg-rolling race.

'Well done,' said Dad.

'What's your prize then?' asked Gran.

'This packet of felt-tips,' said Foxy. 'Isn't it enormous? Do you see, Betsy? You know what they're for, don't you?'

Betsy's eyes lit up.

'Underershed,' she beamed.

'And here's the famous tortoise egg,' said Foxy, pulling it from his pocket. 'You'd never guess that it could beat all those other eggs in the school, would you?'

He held out the cracked, sludge-coloured egg on the palm of his hand.

'Mmm,' said Dad. 'It certainly doesn't look like a champion.'

'It must have been the way I boiled it,' said Mum.

Margaret Joy

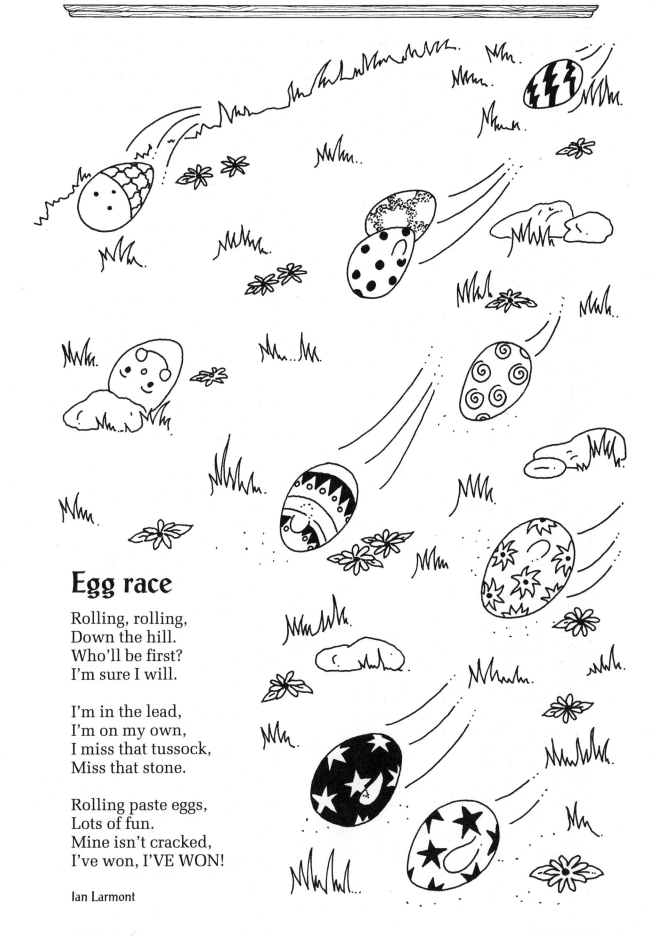

Egg race

Rolling, rolling,
Down the hill.
Who'll be first?
I'm sure I will.

I'm in the lead,
I'm on my own,
I miss that tussock,
Miss that stone.

Rolling paste eggs,
Lots of fun.
Mine isn't cracked,
I've won, I'VE WON!

Ian Larmont

Easter day

Awake! Awake! Jesus has risen!
Today has banished the darkness of night.
A rainbow on high
Crosses the sky
And fills the whole world with colour and light.

A tiny chick pecks its way out of the shell
A shower of rain freshens and cleanses the land.
Rivers are flowing,
Saplings are growing,
Gleaming new shells are washed up on the sand.

A chrysalis grows into a fine butterfly.
Seedlings are pushing their way through the ground.
Gone is the storm,
It is lovely and warm
And lambs that were lost have now all been found.

Daffodils turn to face the bright sun.
Trees sway for joy on this memorable morn.
Birds on the wing
Endlessly sing
To a mother who cradles her baby new-born.

Bob Docherty

The first Easter

One heard in the distance a metallic sound,
Of clattering hooves upon the ground,
As a throng of people now prepare,
To watch the Messiah passing there.

Palm fisted children hurry behind,
They'll follow for ever they do not mind,
Cloaks are strewn across the road,
The donkey stumbles beneath its load.

But soon the Pharisees his death do plan,
Alleging he blasphemed this holy man,
'You said in three days the temple you'd build,'
But to their false accusations he did not yield.

When they took him to Pilate he was aware of his fate,
Their faces were ugly; their eyes filled with hate,
'What am I to do with this Jesus?' he cried,
'Drag him from here to be crucified.'

And so it happened, he hung on a tree,
His mother was crying, his pain there to see,
So a wine soured sponge was held on a rod,
Truly this man was the Son of God.

Then his body was placed in a tomb,
Cut out of rock, he lay in the gloom,
But on the third day he rose once again,
Victory over death was now his claim.

Janet E. Greenyer

The triumph of the witch

'Can't you get to sleep either?' said Susan.

'No,' said Lucy. 'I thought you were asleep. I say, Susan!'

'What?'

'I've a most horrible feeling – as if something were hanging over us.'

'Have you? Because, as a matter of fact, so have I.'

'Something about Aslan,' said Lucy. 'Either some dreadful thing that is going to happen to him, or something dreadful that he's going to do.'

'There's been something wrong with him all afternoon,' said Susan. 'Lucy! What was that he said about not being with us at the battle? You don't think he could be stealing away and leaving us to-night, do you?'

'Where is he now?' said Lucy. 'Is he here in the pavilion?'

'I don't think so.'

'Susan! Let's go outside and have a look round. We might see him.'

'All right. Let's,' said Susan, 'we might just as well be doing that as lying awake here.'

Very quietly the two girls groped their way among the other sleepers and crept out of the tent. The moonlight was bright and everything was quite still except for the noise of the river chattering over the stones. Then Susan suddenly caught Lucy's arm and said, 'Look!' On the far side of the camping ground, just when the trees began, they saw the Lion slowly walking away from them into the wood. Without a word they both followed him.

He led them up the steep slope out of the river valley and then slightly to the right – apparently by the very same route which they had used that afternoon in coming from the Hill of the Stone Table. On and on he led them, into dark shadows and out into pale moonlight, getting their feet wet with the heavy dew. He looked somehow different from the Aslan they knew. His tail and his head hung low and he walked slowly as if he were very, very tired. Then, when they were crossing a wide open place where there were no shadows for them to hide in, he stopped and looked round. It was no good trying to run away so they came towards him.

When they were closer he said, 'Oh children, children, why are you following me?'

'We couldn't sleep,' said Lucy – and then felt sure that she need say no more and that Aslan knew all they had been thinking.

'Please, may we come with you – wherever you're going?' said Susan.

'Well –' said Aslan, and seemed to be thinking. Then he said, 'I should be glad of company to-night. Yes, you may come, if you will promise to stop when I tell you, and after that leave me to go on alone.'

'Oh, thank you, thank you. And we will,' said the two girls.

Forward they went again and one of the girls walked on each side of the Lion. But how slowly he walked! And his great, royal head drooped so that his nose nearly touched the grass. Presently he stumbled and gave a low moan.

'Aslan! Dear Aslan!' said Lucy, 'what is wrong? Can't you tell us?'

'Are you ill, dear Aslan?' asked Susan.

'No,' said Aslan. 'I am sad and lonely. Lay your hands on my mane so that I can feel you are there and let us walk like that.'

And so the girls did what they would never have dared to do without his permission, but what they had longed to do ever since they first saw him – buried their cold hands in the beautiful sea of fur and stroked it and, so doing, walked with him. And presently they saw that they were going with him up the slope of the hill on which the Stone Table stood. They went up at the side where the trees came furthest up, and when they got to the last tree (it was one that had some bushes about it) Aslan stopped and said,

'Oh children, children. Here you must stop. And whatever happens, do not let yourselves be seen. Farewell.'

And both girls cried bitterly (though they hardly knew why) and clung to the Lion and kissed his mane and his nose and his paws and his great, sad eyes. Then he turned from them and walked out on to the top of the hill. And Lucy and Susan, crouching in the bushes, looked after him, and this is what they saw.

A great crowd of people were standing all round the Stone Table and though the moon was shining many of them carried torches which burned with evil-looking red flames and black smoke. But such people! Ogres with monstrous teeth, and wolves, and bull-headed-men; spirits of evil trees and poisonous plants; and other creatures whom I won't describe because if I did the grown-ups would probably not let you read this book – Cruels and Hags and Incubuses, Wraiths, Horrors, Efreets, Sprites, Orknies, Wooses, and Ettins. In fact here were all those who were on the Witch's side and whom the Wolf had summoned at her command. And right in the middle, standing by the Table, was the Witch herself.

A howl and a gibber of dismay went up from the creatures when they first saw the great Lion pacing towards them, and for a moment even the Witch seemed to be struck with fear. Then she recovered herself and gave a wild fierce laugh.

'The fool!' she cried. 'The fool has come. Bind him fast.'

Lucy and Susan held their breaths waiting for Aslan's roar and his spring upon his enemies. But it never came. Four Hags, grinning and leering, yet also (at first) hanging back and half afraid of what they had to do, had approached him. 'Bind him, I say!' repeated the White Witch. The Hags made a dart at him and shrieked with triumph when they found that he made no resistance at all. The others – evil dwarfs and apes – rushed in to help them, and between them they rolled the huge Lion over on his back and tied all his four paws together, shouting and cheering as if they had done something brave, though, had the Lion chosen, one of those paws could have been the death of them all. But he made no noise, even when the enemies, straining and tugging, pulled the cords so tight that they cut into his flesh. Then they began to drag him towards the Stone Table.

'Stop!' said the Witch. 'Let him first be shaved.'

Another roar of mean laughter went up from her followers as an ogre with a pair of shears came forward and squatted down by Aslan's head. Snip-snip-snip went the shears and masses of curling gold began to fall to the ground. Then the ogre stood back and the children, watching from their hiding-place, could see the face of Aslan looking all small and different without its mane. The enemies also saw the difference.

'Why, he's only a great cat after all!' cried one.

'Is *that* what we were afraid of?' said another.

And they surged round Aslan jeering at him, saying things like 'Puss, Puss, Poor Pussy,' and 'How many mice have you caught to-day, Cat?' and 'Would you like a saucer of milk, Pussums?'

'Oh, how *can* they?' said Lucy, tears streaming down her cheeks. 'The brutes, the brutes!' for now that the first shock was over, the shorn face of Aslan looked to her braver, and more beautiful, and more patient than ever.

'Muzzle him!' said the Witch. And even now, as they worked about his face putting on the muzzle, one bite from his jaws would have cost two or three of them their hands. But he never moved. And this seemed to enrage all that rabble. Everyone was at him now. Those who had been afraid to come near him even after he was bound began to find their courage, and for a few minutes the two girls could not even see him – so thickly was he surrounded by the whole crowd of creatures kicking him, hitting him, spitting on him, jeering at him.

At last the rabble had had enough of this. They began to drag the bound and muzzled Lion to the Stone Table, some pulling and some pushing. He was so huge that even when they got him there it took all their effort to hoist him on to the surface of it. Then there was more tying and tightening of cords.

'The cowards! The cowards!' sobbed Susan. 'Are they *still* afraid of him, even now?'

When once Aslan had been tied (and tied so that he was really a mass of cords) on the flat stone, a hush fell on the crowd. Four Hags, holding four torches, stood at the corners of the Table. The Witch bared her arms as she had bared them the previous night when it had been Edmund instead of Aslan. Then she began to whet her knife. It looked to the children, when the gleam of the torchlight fell on it, as if the knife were made of stone, not of steel, and it was of a strange evil shape.

At last she drew near. She stood by Aslan's head. Her face was working and twitching with passion, but his looked up at the sky, still quiet, neither angry, nor afraid, but a little sad. Then, just before she gave the blow, she stooped down and said in a quivering voice,

'And now, who has won? Fool, did you think that by all this you would save the human traitor? Now I will kill you instead of him as our pact was and so the Deep Magic will be appeased. But when you are dead what will prevent me from killing him as well? And who will take him out of my hand *then*? Understand that you have given me Narnia forever, you have lost your own life and you have not saved his. In that knowledge, despair and die.'

The children did not see the actual moment of the killing. They couldn't bear to look and had covered their eyes.

C. S. Lewis

BAISAKHI

Though originally a new year festival for some Hindus, Baisakhi (or Vaisakhi), which falls on 13th April, is now celebrated by Sikhs as the anniversary of the founding of the Khalsa by the tenth Guru, Gobind Singh.

The festival lasts for three days. Sikh baptismal ceremonies are carried out on the third day. New members drink a special amrit (sugar crystals in water) and receive the five Ks. The Guru Granth Sahib is read continuously over the three days, finishing on the morning of the third day. This is known as Akhand Path. At the end of the reading the congregation gathers at the gurdwara for hymns, prayers and to share fruit and Karah prashad before going home to a vegetarian meal.

In the Punjab, Baisakhi is also a harvest celebration and Bhangra dances are performed all over the state.

Manjit goes to the mela

Manjit woke up early in the morning. He was very excited. Today was Baisakhi. There would be a big mela in the town. Manjit remembered that last year he had watched the juggler and the magicians. He had bought a little clay doll from the toy-seller for his sister. He had tasted barfi and laddus. He had ridden on the Ferris wheel. He had enjoyed the performing puppets.

He leapt out of bed and drank his lassi. He was so excited that he could not keep still. 'Hurry up Mum, hurry up Dad, we're going to miss all the fun.'

'We won't be ready for a while yet. I've milked the buffalo and swept the yard but I must prepare the food for tonight,' said Mum.

'Yes, and I have to harvest the wheat today before I can go and enjoy myself at the mela,' said Dad. 'You go on and we'll see you at the mela.'

Manjit picked up his money bag and counted his rupees. What could he spend it on, he wondered as he dashed out of the house.

Not far from the village he saw a boy with a long wooden pole over his shoulder from which brightly coloured balloons were blowing in the wind. There were long blue ones,

round yellow ones and green and red stripy ones. Manjit ran after him and caught him up. 'Where are you going?' said Manjit to the balloon boy.

'I'm off to the fair to sell my balloons. Why don't you come with me?'

'My sister would love one of those yellow balloons,' said Manjit. He bought one straight away. Manjit and the balloon boy walked on together.

After a few minutes they came across a man sitting in the shade of a mango tree by the roadside. He had a wooden box with him. 'Hullo there,' said the man. 'Can I walk with you? I'm going your way.'

'Where are you going?' said Manjit to the man. 'I'm off to the fair to sell my toys.'

'Oh what have you got? Can I look inside your box?' The man threw back the lid. Inside were gaily painted clay dolls, clockwork peacocks, spinning tops with rainbow patterns and carved wooden elephants.

'Can I buy one of those elephants for my brother?' asked Manjit. Then Manjit, the balloon boy and the toy-seller walked on together.

At the crossroads they met a man with a bundle on his head.

'Hullo,' called Manjit. 'Where are you going?'

'I'm going to the fair to perform for the crowd. I can juggle five balls at once or balance an egg on the end of my nose while walking on my hands.'

'Oh, I wish I could do that.' Manjit and the balloon boy and the toy-seller and the juggler walked on together.

At the top of the hill they saw two men pushing a hand-cart. Manjit ran up to look in the cart.

'Where are you going?' said Manjit.

'We're going to the fair to do our puppet play. It's the story of Heer Rarjah. Will you come and watch us at the fair?' So Manjit and the balloon boy and the toy-seller and the juggler and the puppeteers all walked on together.

Ahead of them they saw a man carrying a covered basket under his arm. He turned his head as he heard them coming.

'Where are you going?' asked Manjit.

'I'm going to the fair to show everyone my incredible tricks. I can make flowers appear out of your hair and coins vanish in a puff of smoke.'

'Will you show my dad when he gets to the fair?' said Manjit. Manjit and the balloon boy and the toy-seller and the juggler and the puppeteers and the magician walked on together.

As they neared the town, Manjit could see the crowds and hear the music. A warm smell of samosas and pokoras reached his nose. The Ferris wheel was turning. Manjit couldn't wait. He turned to his friends and shouted 'See you later' as he ran along the road and was lost in the crowd.

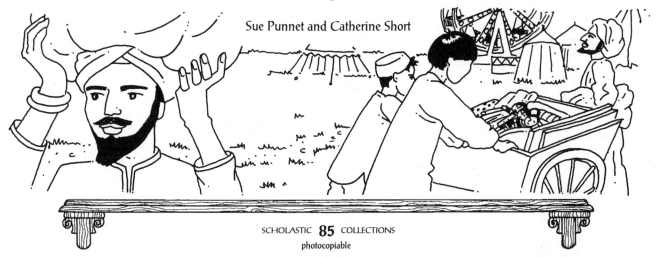

Sue Punnet and Catherine Short

Festival of harvest

Baisakhi the festival of the harvest,
Is celebrated in Punjab with traditional gaiety and jest.
It is a time to cut the crops sown deep in the soil,
And to bear fruits of the farmer's hard toil.
It marks the beginning of the farmer's New Year,
And is a time to enjoy and feast with his near and dear.
To dance all his cares away,
To just be happy and gay.
But in my golden Punjab, in the recent past,
Baisakhi has always had a blood-bath.
Fighting and arson, killing and tension,
Are just a few incidents to mention.
I earnestly pray that this Baisakhi may be the day,
When we all rise and say, we shall fight out all enmity,
And in this golden land bring peace and amity.

Ruchi Chatterji, aged 16

Vaisakhi is here

The season of golden fields
and heaps of grain.
Love and affection
and brotherhood.

Farms, factories,
mandis and bazaars
bustle with
business activity.
The valiant sons of Punjab,
vigorous as ever,
dancing to the beat
of bhangra.
And the young damsels
moving to the tune of giddha.
The entire country
rejoices with them.

THIS IS WHAT
WE ARE CELEBRATING TODAY –
THE SPIRIT OF PUNJAB
AND ITS NATURAL RHYTHM.

Anonymous

The story of Baisakhi

Baisakhi Day is celebrated in many parts of India, but for Sikhs it is an especially important festival. This story tells why.

It was springtime and Guru Gobind Singh had called his followers together for the festival of Baisakhi. The scent of spring flowers filled the air as his followers hurried up the hilltop to the fortress castle of Anandpur. There, a large tent had been set up. There was an excited hubbub as the people gathered around.

Suddenly the crowd fell silent as Guru Gobind Singh strode out on stage in front of the tent, an unsheathed sword in his hand. Everyone waited expectantly.

'Is there anyone among you who would lay down his life for God and his Guru?' he cried, looking at the crowd below him.

There was a shocked pause; no one spoke.

'Is there anyone among you who would lay down his life for God and his Guru?' his voice rang out, more loudly this time.

The people in the crowd turned to each other in disbelief. 'Has he called us here to die?' they asked one another. 'Surely he isn't serious.'

The Guru waited, imposingly. Then one man moved forward out of the crowd. His name was Daya Ram. 'I would willingly lay down my life for my God and my Guru,' he said steadily, looking at the Guru.

'Come with me,' replied the Guru and led him into the tent. The people watching held their breath. Suddenly there was a whoosh, then a thud. Guru Gobind Singh returned to the crowd, holding his sword in the air. It seemed to be dripping with blood. They all watched, stunned.

'Who will be next?' he cried. 'Who else will lay down his life for God and his Guru?'

The people were horrified. Why was their Guru doing this?

'I will willingly lay down my life for God and my Guru,' came a second voice from the crowd. Another man stepped forward.

The Guru led him into the tent. Again they heard a whoosh, followed by a thud. Once more the Guru reappeared with his sword apparently dripping with blood.

But the horror had not finished. Three times more the Guru asked the people his terrible question. Each time another volunteer came forward. The Guru disappeared into the tent with him and then returned to the crowd alone. Each time the crowd heard the terrible noise and saw what looked like a bloodstained sword. It was too much. The people watching were so shocked that many started running away in fear, sobbing.

Suddenly the Guru's voice could be heard above the terrified cries. 'Wait!' he called. 'Don't go! I have something to show you.' The people stopped and some started turning back. The Guru disappeared into the tent. A few minutes later he returned leading all five men, their hair neatly tied in turbans. The crowd gasped in disbelief. How could these men be alive? The Guru spoke:

'You all had so little faith, except for these five men. They alone have shown a very special kind of bravery. I will call these men the blessed five.'

The Guru pointed to the men standing next to him:

'I want all Sikhs to be brave and fearless like they were. We will form a brotherhood called the Khalsa. Everyone will be equal and we will all share the same name. Sikh men will be called Singh (which means lion) and Sikh women will be called Kaur (which means princess).

'So that people know we are Sikhs, we will wear special signs. We will wear our hair uncut, tied up and kept in place with a small comb and covered by a turban. On our wrists we will wear a steel bangle, because steel stands for strength and courage. We will carry a sword to protect the weak and ourselves. So that we can ride our horses with ease, we will wear special trousers. We will learn to live, work and play together as equals. With our special appearance we cannot hide anywhere in the world. We will always be noticed for what we do.'

Then the Guru blessed the men. He took a bowl of sweetened holy water call amrit and stirred it with a small sword. He gave the five some of this water to drink and then sprinkled it over their heads. As he did so he made them members of the new family, the Khalsa. It is said that at the end of the day over 20,000 people became members in this way.

Rani and Jugnu Singh

WESAK

Wesak is celebrated on the full moon day in the month of Vesakha, or Vaisakha, (April–May).

This is the main Buddhist festival when Theravada Buddhists in Burma, Thailand and Sri Lanka celebrate the birth (in 563BCE), enlightenment (in 528BCE) and the death (in 483BCE) of Gautama Buddha. The festival lasts for three days and houses, temples and statues of the Buddha are decorated with flowers and lights. Presents are exchanged and gifts given to the poor as a symbol of the Buddha's concern and compassion for humankind; caged birds are released in memory of his love for all living things.

Mahayana Buddhists celebrate the birth of the Buddha as a separate festival.

Prince Siddhartha is born

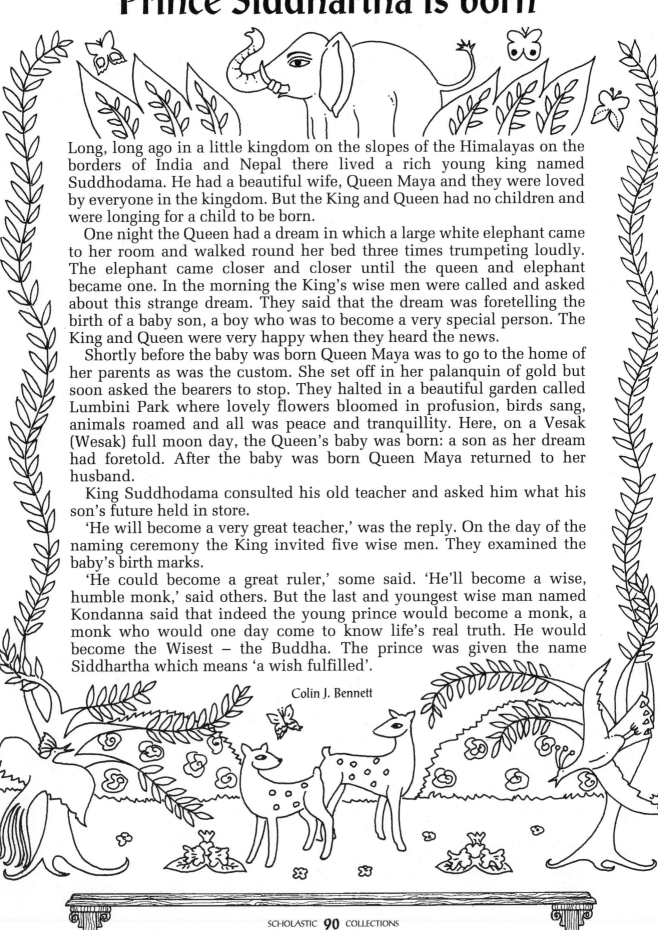

Long, long ago in a little kingdom on the slopes of the Himalayas on the borders of India and Nepal there lived a rich young king named Suddhodama. He had a beautiful wife, Queen Maya and they were loved by everyone in the kingdom. But the King and Queen had no children and were longing for a child to be born.

One night the Queen had a dream in which a large white elephant came to her room and walked round her bed three times trumpeting loudly. The elephant came closer and closer until the queen and elephant became one. In the morning the King's wise men were called and asked about this strange dream. They said that the dream was foretelling the birth of a baby son, a boy who was to become a very special person. The King and Queen were very happy when they heard the news.

Shortly before the baby was born Queen Maya was to go to the home of her parents as was the custom. She set off in her palanquin of gold but soon asked the bearers to stop. They halted in a beautiful garden called Lumbini Park where lovely flowers bloomed in profusion, birds sang, animals roamed and all was peace and tranquillity. Here, on a Vesak (Wesak) full moon day, the Queen's baby was born: a son as her dream had foretold. After the baby was born Queen Maya returned to her husband.

King Suddhodama consulted his old teacher and asked him what his son's future held in store.

'He will become a very great teacher,' was the reply. On the day of the naming ceremony the King invited five wise men. They examined the baby's birth marks.

'He could become a great ruler,' some said. 'He'll become a wise, humble monk,' said others. But the last and youngest wise man named Kondanna said that indeed the young prince would become a monk, a monk who would one day come to know life's real truth. He would become the Wisest – the Buddha. The prince was given the name Siddhartha which means 'a wish fulfilled'.

Colin J. Bennett

Lotus

The beautiful lotus is rather like a water lily. The plant is rooted in mud but pushes up towards the light and flowers on the surface of the water. During Wesak lotus buds are offered at shrines to celebrate the birth and enlightenment of Gautama Buddha.

Though each of my roots
in darkness was born
yet will I reach for the light,
yet will I rise to the sun.

Judith Nicholls

The birds

Bring out the bird cage!
Open the door –
let the captive
fly...
Into the unlocked air
he goes,
into the open
sky
lurching and soaring
in his joy,
perching on branch
and tree,
bursting his throat
to tell the world
that now, at last,
he's free!

Jean Kenward

Wesak

The great full moon of May is come,
and Wesak's in the air.
Have you hung the lantern out
and put a candle there?
Have you gathered flowers
to decorate the shrine
with leaves and blossom freshly picked?
(Come and look at mine!)

The great full moon of May rolls on
from sunset until dawn...
We celebrate the joyful day
Buddha himself was born.
We celebrate the truth he learned
under the holy tree,
and try and live as he would live –
and be what he would be.

Jean Kenward

Wesak

Full moon in May,
Buddha's birthday.
Enlightenment gained.
Nirvana attained.
Gifts for the poor,
Flowers round the door.
So streets decorate,
And all celebrate!

Wendy P. Larmont

Awakening

The Buddha sat under
the Bodhi tree.
He sat and he waited
determinedly.

He sat like a statue
and scarcely stirred.
Out of his lips
came never a word.

He sat through the hours
of an Orient night,
and just at the edges
of opening light

Up in the heaven
so sharp and so far
glimmered the spark
of a wakening star.

Sitting in stillness
the sight that he saw
pierced him through
to the innermost core.

And all he could say
in that great clarity
was simply and purely
'What can this be?'

Tony Mitton

Buddha Lord we offer

Adaptation and music by Dr June Tillman

2. Holy Day of Wesak,
Day of Buddha's birth,
When the sun of wisdom
Shone upon the earth.

3. Incense too we offer
On this Festal Day,
For the things we cherish
All must pass away.

4. Through this holy symbol,
We shall learn to see,
Things of priceless value
Hid in transiency.

5. And the deep gong sounding
Bids us leave the self,
And in Buddha's teaching
Find the truest wealth.

6. Lights upon the altar
Show to us the way,
Find the realms of darkness
To Nirvana's day.

RAKSHA BANDHAN

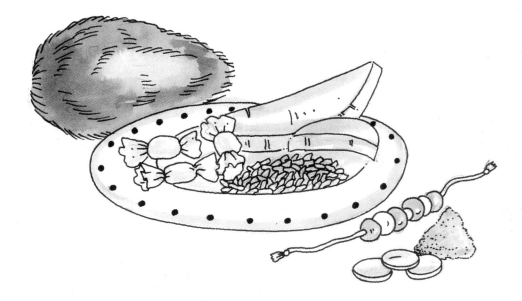

This festival, often called the 'rakhi festival' is celebrated on the last of Sawan (Shravan) and was said to be instituted in honour of the good genie when Sage Durvasas instructed Salona, the nymph presiding over the month of Sawan, to bind rakhis as charms to avert evil.

It is essentially a festival of brothers and sisters but Brahmins may tie rakhis to their protectors, the Kshatriyas. The symbolic meaning of tying a rakhi is to seek protection.

The festival was thought to have started during medieval times when there was much looting and rape. In order to protect themselves women tied rakhis to their brothers; a woman might also make some brave warrior a brother by the tying of a rakhi. He in return then had to vow to protect her with his life.

The tying of a rakhi has another meaning too. When a sister ties a rakhi she also prays for the long life of her brother, 'May this rakhi protect you from all harm and so protect me from all harm.' A sister will often put on her best clothes and, taking a plate decorated with vermilion, rice grains, coconut, sweets, a rakhi and some money, go to visit her brother. He sits before her and she first marks a tilak on his forehead on to which she places a few grains of rice. She then ties the rakhi, places a sweet into his mouth and puts the coconut and money into his hands. The brother in return may give some money and clothes. (Clothing is thought of as a symbol of protection.)

Nowadays many school children make rakhis and tie them to each other to show their love and affection.

There are many other stories about the origin of rakhis.

A Krishna story for Raksha Bandhan

Long, long ago, so the story goes, Krishna had two sisters. One, his sister by birth, was named Subhadra and the other, Draupadi, was really an adopted sister. Krishna loved both his sisters and treated them in exactly the same way.

Now Subhadra was not a happy girl and she didn't like Draupadi. She was very jealous and whenever Krishna played with her Subhadra would try to stop their fun. 'It's not fair,' Subhadra complained to Krishna, 'You're MY brother. I am your real sister. Draupadi's not our proper sister; you should play with me. You ought to love me more that you love her. You know I love you more than she does.'

This made Draupadi unhappy for she loved Krishna dearly. Krishna too felt sad as he loved both sisters and he worried about Subhadra's jealousy.

Then one day Subhadra's love was tested. Krishna cut his hand and the blood would not stop; it was going everywhere. Subhadra came into the room and Krishna held out his hand to her. 'Ugh! I hate the sight of blood and it's going all over the place,' she cried and hurried off leaving Krishna still trying to stop the dripping blood.

Soon Draupadi came in. She too saw the blood. 'Oh! Poor Krishna,' she said, 'look at your hand. I must do something.' And with that she tore a strip of cloth from her sari and used it to bind up the cut.

Krishna sat down feeling quite weak from the loss of blood and as he rested he said to himself, 'How kind and thoughtful Draupadi is. Now I hope Subhadra will understand why I love her like a real sister.'

Renuka Singh

Indra and Indrana

This story tells of the king of heaven, Indra, who was beaten by the demon Bali and driven away from his kingdom.

Indra was unable to protect himself from the evil demon and, feeling humiliated, hid himself away, but his consort Sachi was determined to help. So, gathering her courage, she went to seek aid from the Great God, Vishnu, the preserver. As she entered his palace Sachi was trembling but remembering Indra's danger she went and stood before Vishnu.

When he heard her tale of woe Vishnu felt sorry for the couple and gave Sachi a powerful thread to tie around her husband's wrist. This thread protected Indra and he was then able to drive the demon away and win back his celestial kingdom.

Renuka Singh

Raksha Bandhan

Shravana brings a special date
When brothers and sisters celebrate.

Sisters weave with silken thread
A bracelet band of gold and red.

Her brother's wrist she ties it round,
A symbol that he now is bound

To promise that he always will
Protect and save her from all ill.

She dabs his brow with powder red,
A sign of great success ahead,

Then families rejoice and pray
And have a happy Rakhi Day.

Wendy P. Larmont

Raksha Bandhan – Brother's day

The stalls are dressed in many colours,
The markets come alive,
The glittering circlets and bracelets of ribbon,
Are tokens for which we strive.

After prayers are softly spoken,
Will our sisters now come by?
Will they tie our wrists with bracelets?
It's an honour we can't deny.

Yes, we've been chosen by our sisters,
We'll protect them from this day,
Then with pride we'll wear our bracelets,
As we go singing on our way.

Janet E. Greenyer

My brother Raja

Sometimes I hate my brother so much; ooh, so much that I wish... I wish I could pull his hair. But he's too strong. I wish I never had to see him again, with his stupid face and sticking-out ears. I wish I were deaf, so I wouldn't have to listen to him. 'Little baby Bina, silly little screamer.' He also says things like, 'Bina the screamer ate a rat, and got very very fat.' Dad says I'm NOT fat, just nicely covered, but my brother makes fun of me all the time.

When Annie came to spend the day last week we played our restaurant game. Mummy lent us lots of things from the kitchen: knives and forks, some small saucepans to cook with, wooden spoons, a rolling pin and a pastry board. She gave us plates and glasses and two empty jam-jars and a bowl. We made a restaurant in the garden with two tables and flowers in the jam-jars. We made chapatis and salad and Angel Delight. Annie and I made a menu with prices and her mum and mine came and ordered a meal. We even had a sign, 'Garden Café', it said.

But after they had gone back inside the house, what do you think happened? That horrible brother of mine came racing down the lawn with our dog, Tinker. They went straight into our tables and knocked them down. There was water everywhere and everything was spoiled. I punched him and got very angry, but he's two years older than me so he didn't feel it much. Then he got angry and twisted my arm in a Chinese bangle and it hurt so much that I started to cry. 'Sorry,' he said when Mummy made him say it. But he mumbled it very fast and when she wasn't looking he stuck his tongue out at me. 'I told you it was an accident,' he said. Then he started singing very softly, 'Cry baby Bina, the silly little screamer.'

In our family we have loads and loads of special days. Once I counted them. Six birthdays: Mummy's, Dad's, mine, my big brother Rahul's, Raja's and Granny's. Festivals: Raksha Bandhan, Diwali, Dussehra, Lori, Holi, so that's five. I can't decide which is my favourite festival. Probably Diwali because of the lights and fireworks and a big party with millions of friends and lovely sweets from a shop in Leicester. But I also like Raksha Bandhan. Granny says this is when it's really fun being a girl. If you have brothers they have to give you money and presents and promise to look after you.

'It's Shravan Purnima, full moon, next Wednesday,' she said at breakfast, 'Raksha Bandhan. I hope you boys have thought about what you're going to give Bina,' she said to Rahul and Raja.

'Why do brothers have to give presents to their sisters?' I asked.

'It's a very old tradition,' Granny explained. 'Hundreds of years ago men folk used to go to war on their horses, with their shields and swords by their side. Their sisters would give them a blessing and put a *tikka* on their foreheads for their safe return. Then, in return, their brothers would promise to look after their sisters. They would give them a gift because they were grateful for their prayers.'

I thought about what Granny said all day long. I wasn't feeling at all friendly towards Raja. He was being horrible to me and Annie at school. He and his gang had told us to beat it because they wanted our corner of the playground for their soccer practice. I'd also found an enormous earwig in my lunch box and I was sure Raja had put it there.

'I'm going on strike,' I told Mummy when I came home from school that day. 'I'm not giving Raja a blessing or tying a rakhi on him at Raksha Bandhan. I'll tie a rakhi on Rahul, but not Raja, and I'm not going to change my mind.'

On the morning of Raksha Bandhan Dad got a rakhi in the post from his sister in India. It was a beautiful gold tinsel bracelet and had purple and green bobbles woven in it. Mummy tied it on his wrist and did a little puja with an oil lamp. Then she put a *tikka* of saffron and rice grains on his forehead and a sweet golden *ladoo* in his mouth.

'What about Aunty Lata's present?' I asked.

'It has been sent already. I sent her a cheque in the post,' he said picking up his paper to go off to work. 'Don't forget to get something nice from your brothers,' he smiled. Mummy's brother was coming over in the evening to have his rakhi tied and to give her his present.

I tied a pretty silver thread bracelet on Rahul's wrist. He was also leaving to go to college. He's very kind and not a bit like Raja. 'Not too much *ladoo*, Bina,' he laughed. 'I've just done my teeth!' He gave me a kiss and a five pound note.

'Thank you, Rahul.' I was really pleased.

'And I promise to look after you always.' He hugged me. 'Now where's that wicked boy Raja?'

I shrugged. 'I don't know and I don't care. I'm on strike,' I said very seriously. 'He's been so awful to me that I won't give him a blessing and I don't want his present.'

'Oh, child, you can't say that,' Granny cried. 'Your brother is your brother and you are his sister. Nothing can change that.'

I ran out of the kitchen, picked up my school-bag and flew out before anyone could say anything else.

Well, it turned out to be the worst day of my life. Mrs Reeves told me off for talking during Silent Reading. I wasn't talking. I just asked Tamsin if I could look at her pencil case. Then I got told off for doing Annie's hair during Story Time. Then I got told off for not listening when Mrs Reeves was telling us about Queen Victoria. Then she said I was creating a disturbance and shouted at me. We all had to sit with our fingers on our lips like babies to keep us quiet and everyone blamed me at playtime. Annie went off without me. I'd left my sandwiches at home. Then one of the helpers told me off.

I felt miserable. I walked round the playground all by myself. I could feel a lump starting in my throat. Then something even worse happened. Tommy Allen from Raja's class came running straight at me. He crashed into me and I fell flat on my bottom and hit my elbow against a concrete flower tub.

'Look where you're going, you silly moron,' he shouted. I didn't know what a moron was, but I knew it was rude. It was too much. I burst into tears and just sat there on the ground with my knees up to my chin and cried and cried. I wasn't making a loud noise or anything, so no one noticed and no one came up to see what was wrong. Normally Annie would have come to my help and then we would have gone together to the dinner lady and told her about Tommy Allen. But Annie was with Sarah and Karen and Surjit. I felt so lonely and miserable.

Suddenly I felt someone come up and touch me on the shoulder.

'What's the matter Bina?' It was Raja. He sat down next to me. 'Come on, Beens, tell me what's happened?' he said in a gentle voice and I started to cry all over again. He got on to his knees and put his arm around me. 'Beens, don't cry. Just tell me what's wrong.'

So I told him about Mrs Reeves and Annie and how I'd forgotten my sandwiches and about Tommy Allen.

'Look, stop crying. I'll go and get Annie and tell Tommy he has to say sorry to you. Here,' he reached inside the pocket of his anorak. He held out a giant-sized chocolate bar. Fruit and nut, my favourite. 'Here's your rakhi present. You forgot to tie it on me this morning.'

I sniffed and blew my nose. I saw him go up to Annie and talk to her. In a few seconds they both came running back.

'We thought you didn't want to play with us,' said Annie. 'Come on,' she pulled me up, 'We've got three teams going.' Raja dusted me down gently. 'All right now?' he said anxiously. I nodded.

I put the chocolate safely into my pocket. I still had to give him his blessing and tie a rakhi and put a *ladoo* in his mouth. I'd do it as soon as we got home in the afternoon.

Pratima Mitchell

The Rakhree

Traditional Punjabi

Starting note: E

Chorus

Bhen ko - lon veer vay bhan - aa - leh ra - khree,

Fine

Soho - nney je - hey gu - tte te se - jaa - leh ra - khree.

1. Ehd - ne wich mer - ri - on mor - a - dan veer vay,

(Chorus)

Shet na - lon mit - ti - on ne ya - dan veer vay.

2. Ehd - ne wich gun - di - ar py - ar ban daa,

(Chorus)

Ehd - ne wich chaar tai ma - lahr bhan daa.

3. Ehd - ne wich pre tan daa ey rang veer - na,

(Chorus)

Ehd - ne wich bhan dee u - mang veer nan.

King Poras keeps his promise

Long, long ago India was ruled by a great and noble king named Poras. In those days India was the richest and most splendid country in the world. Her people were prosperous and contented, many wore beautiful clothes and some lived in fine marble palaces.

Because of the gold and precious jewels that were rumoured to be in India, all the world's rulers wanted to own her. The greatest of these was Alexander, the emperor of the Greeks. Alexander was a fine warrior who had conquered many countries, and wanted to rule the entire world. He had set his heart on conquering India.

Poras too was a great warrior. He was also a good and kind ruler, and was determined never to allow his country to be invaded by another.

Now there was a woman Alexander loved, a beautiful Persian princess with blue eyes called Rukhsana. When she realised that he was set on conquering India, she was afraid, for King Poras' army was known to be strong and powerful. She decided to follow her beloved secretly to India, fearing for his life.

Wearing a veil over her face so that nobody could see that she was not an Indian woman, Rukhsana crossed the frontier and made her way to the city where Poras had his great palace. As she arrived there, she heard the sound of merrymaking and laughter in the streets.

'Please, tell me what the celebrations are for?' she said to an old man who was passing.

'Don't you know, my dear, that today we are celebrating the Festival of Rakhee?' he replied. When she shook her head, he went on, 'Rakhee means protection, and today is the day when sisters tie a special string on their brothers' wrists, and in return the brothers promise to protect them and grant them whatever they want. It is a most sacred and important day! Why don't you join in the festivities?'

But Rukhsana had already disappeared into the crowd, for a clever idea had struck her while the old man was speaking. She bought a rakhee string from the bazaar and then hurried to the palace. Entering the gates, she passed through many splendid rooms crowded with people in fine clothes. At last she came to the great hall, and there she saw the mighty ruler sitting on his throne, surrounded by his courtiers.

Rukhsana removed her veil and everyone stared as the beautiful and mysterious lady walked straight up to the king and tied the rakhee string on his wrist. There was silence in the hall.

At last Poras spoke. 'Lady, you have the bluest eyes I have ever seen. You must come from some far off place. Who are you?' Rukhsana did not reply.

'Well,' said Poras, with this rakhee you have made me your brother. Whatever you wish for, it will be granted.'

Then, holding her head high, Rukhsana spoke. 'I ask you for the life of the emperor Alexander,' she said. 'He has come to this land to do battle with you, but I want you, as my brother, to promise that he will never be killed by your hand.'

Now Indian rulers placed much importance on their word and their promise. It was a matter of great honour, and Poras paused for a moment.

He looked at the proud and brave lady and replied, 'Yes, oh fair one. You have tied this rakhee on me, and I have promised to grant your wish. I will do as you ask.'

The courtiers looked in amazement, but Poras held up his hand to show that he had given his word. Rukhsana bowed her head in gratitude to the noble ruler who sat before her, then turned and walked out of the palace.

Meanwhile, Alexander had crossed the Indian frontier and was marching inland at the head of his conquering army. However, his progress was not easy, for Poras' soldiers were well-trained and fearless, and everywhere there were scenes of fierce fighting and bloodshed.

At last, Poras himself drew up his mighty army of elephants, horses and men on the banks of a river, and prepared to face the invader in a great battle. Alexander the Great, wearing shining armour, rode at the head of his army on a snow-white horse. Poras rode on a huge elephant decked in gold and jewels. After many attempts Alexander and his men succeeded in crossing the river and attacking. The battle which followed raged for many hours with hundreds of men killed or wounded on both sides.

Eventually, Poras and Alexander drew up close to each other on their mounts, and prepared to fight man to man. All around the men stopped and stared. Soldiers moved away to make space for the two great rulers to fight. A hush over both armies as everyone watched and waited.

The two men turned about and rode hard towards each other, spurring on their steeds. They rode closer and closer, thundering across the ground which was wet and soft after the heavy monsoon rains.

Suddenly Alexander's horse slipped in some mud and its legs buckled, throwing the emperor forward on to the ground. The mighty conqueror was helpless. Poras raised his arm to throw his sharp spear at Alexander, he could hardly miss at this close range. But then he remembered his promise to Rukhsana. He had given his word of honour that Alexander would never die at his hand, the hand on which Rukhsana had tied a rakhee.

Poras' generals and soldiers watched, amazed, as Poras lowered his spear, turned his elephant and rode away.

And that is how Alexander the Great was saved from death by a promise – the word of honour which Poras gave to Rukhsana when she tied a rakhee bracelet on his wrist. In fact, the battle was finally won by Alexander but he could see that Poras was a fine and honourable king so he offered the Indian ruler a treaty. The two men became sound allies, and each admired the other greatly for his bravery, skills and noble character.

Rakhee is still celebrated in the month of August by Indians all over the world. Sisters tie an elegant bracelet on those whom they call their brothers, and in return their brothers promise them eternal protection and loyalty.

Rani Singh

JANMASHTAMI

This Hindu festival marks the birthday of Lord Krishna, the eighth incarnation of Vishnu and falls on the eighth day of Shravan (between July and September).

The celebration begins at midnight, the time of Krishna's birth, and a fast is observed all day until that hour when conch shells are blown and bells rung. Just before midnight a statue of the baby Krishna is washed with yoghurt, ghee, sugar, milk and honey. This is collected and shared as a special drink for everyone. A statue or picture of Lord Krishna is placed in a beautifully decorated cradle or swing which is rocked to amuse the infant. At midnight the arti ceremony is performed. A celebration feast is held but no meat or grain is eaten at the meal.

Krishna is born

Once upon a time, when India was a land of magic and maharajahs, there was a little kingdom on the banks of the Yamuna River. Every spring the fast-flowing waters of this river in northern India were fed by melting Himalayan snow. The land all around the Yamuna was lush and green, rich and fertile. The people of Mathura farmed, traded and prospered; and every year they made sacrifices to thank the gods for their good fortune.

Life would have been perfect for these good and hard-working people had it not been for their King. The Maharajah of Mathura, whose name was Kans, was known far and wide as a monster. When he was young, he had wanted to be King so much that he was prepared to do anything. Rather than wait, as a dutiful son should, to inherit the throne, he plotted to overthrow his father so that he could be King instead. The citizens of Mathura were terrified of Kans because he did exactly as he pleased, often killing or imprisoning people just because he didn't like them.

Kans' father Ugrasen had always been kind and just to his people, whilst Kans had never shown them any kindness even as a young boy. He had always behaved as if it was his right to walk into any house or shop and demand whatever he wanted. He pestered girls from respectable families and when their parents hid them away, he had their homes destroyed. For a while the people of Mathura had felt powerless to do anything. Finally, things became so bad that a group of merchants decided to complain.

The old King of Mathura regularly held court at his palace where he listened to complaints, resolved quarrels and generally helped his people in whatever way he could. At these courts, even the most humble street-sweeper knew that he would be listened to with respect, and that he could speak freely without fear of punishment. The merchants decided that this court was the place to make their complaint. As usual, the courtroom was full of people. There was hardly room to stand. The merchants waited for their turn to speak, and when it came, they stood up together. They were trembling and wringing their hands nervously. They knew that their King was a fair and just man, but what would he do when he heard complaints against his own son?

The King saw at once that the merchants were afraid and he spoke to them kindly.

'Speak freely, my good merchants,' he said. 'Tell me what is worrying you. A King is a father to his people, and like a good father, I am here to listen to your problems, whatever they may be.'

At this, the merchants felt more confident, and their leader began to speak.

'Sire, you are indeed like a father to us. We love you as a son loves his father, and we have always felt that we could come to you whenever we have needed help and advice but....'

'Speak, my dear man, speak,' said the old King graciously.

'Well, Sire, it's about Prince Kans,' said the merchant. 'We have tried to be understanding and we don't mind giving him presents, but, Sire, we are not rich, and now even our daughters are not safe....'

Ugrasen didn't need to hear any more. This was just what he had always suspected. He had tried to teach his son how to behave by setting a good example, but now he knew that he had failed. Even the wise men who had taught Kans as a boy had not been able to control his mean and cruel nature. The old man shook his head and sighed sadly. He was ashamed to hear his subjects complaining about his own son, but in all fairness, he knew they would not have complained without proper cause.

'I have heard your complaint and I promise you that my son Kans will not bother you or your daughters again,' he said. 'Court dismissed.'

The King left the courtroom and ordered his sentries to bring Kans to him at once. He began pacing the floor impatiently but before long he heard footsteps tramping down the passage. The door flew open and Kans marched in, followed by the sentries. Every man had his sword drawn and pointed at the old King.

'What is the meaning of this?' demanded Ugrasen.

'Can't you guess, Father?' sneered Kans. 'It means that these men are under my orders and they will do as I tell them.' He turned to the sentries. 'Take him away to the dungeons, and make sure that I never see him again!' he ordered.

The awful news of what Kans had done soon spread throughout the little kingdom. It was the worst thing that could have happened to the people of Mathura. They had dared to complain about Kans, and now he was their King instead. From now on he had the power to make life twice as difficult for them.

It was just as they had predicted. Within days, Kans' soldiers were seen in every street. They looted shops and houses and threatened innocent people. His spies were everywhere. Any person heard complaining about Kans was immediately imprisoned or killed. People began to disappear never to return, and soon the very air in Mathura smelt of fear.

As the years went by Kans became more and more cruel, and although the people of Mathura were well fed and clothed, their life became a misery. They lived in constant fear and no one could tell when Kans' evil eye would fall upon them. It seemed as though even the gods to whom they prayed every morning and evening had forsaken them.

The people of Mathura did not know it, but Prithvi, the Earth goddess, had been watching her people's suffering for some time. Her temples were filled with men and women begging for help. Each day, the temples echoed with the sound of their cries, which became more desperate as the days passed. Powerless to do anything by herself, Prithvi turned to the other gods and goddesses for help.

Up in the heavens above the highest mountains in the land, Indra, the King of Heaven, already knew about Kans' reign of terror. Hearing Prithvi's call, he summoned Brahma the Creator, Vishnu the Preserver and the Good, and Shiva the Destroyer of the Universe. Together they would surely be able to think of a plan to destroy Kans. Although they were gods, they could not meddle in the affairs of mortals on Earth unless they themselves took the form of mortals. The gods decided that only Vishnu's powers of good could fight Kans' evil.

'Have faith,' said Indra to Prithvi. 'We know how the people of Mathura have suffered, and soon, a child will be born on Earth who will rid Mathura of its evil King.'

Reassured by Indra's words, Prithvi returned to Earth to wait for the coming of the miracle child.

Kans had a younger sister called Devaki who was different in every way from her brother. Devaki was a quiet and gentle princess who was as kind as Kans was cruel, and humble as he was proud. When Devaki grew old enough to marry, Kans made sure that she would marry a man from outside Mathura. He wanted to make sure that if Devaki had sons, they would not be able to claim his throne from him. Devaki had been terrified of her brother all her young life, and she was happy enough at the thought of leaving Mathura forever. Kans was so pleased at the thought of ridding himself of his sister that he planned a very grand wedding indeed.

As dawn broke on the wedding day, the streets of Mathura were already decorated with streamers of mango leaves and sweet-smelling frangipani and jasmine flowers. Kans ordered his court musicians to play their loudest and most joyful music, and sent servants out into his kingdom to deliver sweets made of milk and ghee, honey and nuts to every family. Each woman was given a sari of glistening silk, and each man a shawl of the finest wool. By the time Devaki's bridegroom, whose name was Vasudev, arrived for the wedding, every face in Mathura was smiling.

Kans was beaming as he watched the priest chanting prayers over the holy fire. Devaki and Vasudev exchanged their marriage vows in front of the fire, which filled the air with the smell of burning sandalwood, ghee and incense. When they finally garlanded each other with flowers and knelt before the priest for his blessing, a tremendous cheer went up in the streets of Mathura. Now everyone knew that Vasudev and Devaki were man and wife.

It was while entertaining his guests at the wedding feast that one of Kans' most trusted servants came to him with a message.

'Sire,' he whispered into Kans' ear, 'there is an old man waiting to see you outside the palace gates. I have told him that you are too busy to see him today, but he refuses to go. He insists that what he has to say is a matter of the utmost importance to you. He says that he has come to warn you.'

'Who would presume to give me, the King, a warning?' wondered Kans. 'I know that people in Mathura hate me, but they wouldn't dare harm me.' Nevertheless, he arranged to meet the man outside the city, away from curious eyes and ears. Kans had been enjoying himself at the feast, indulging his love of good food and drink, and he was not pleased to have to leave it. As he hurried to meet the man, Kans began to wonder if he was walking into a trap. He felt suspicious, and he was in a very bad mood by the time he reached the meeting-place.

The old man was sitting under a large peepul tree where he had been ordered to wait. He was sitting cross-legged, murmuring a prayer with his eyes closed. In his thin, wrinkled old hands he held a string of fragrant sandalwood prayer beads. As he prayed, he seemed to be counting the beads, picking at each one slowly.

Most people would have waited for the old man to finish his prayers but Kans was not used to being kept waiting. He was already irritated at having to leave the feast, and he marched up to the man.

'What do you want, old man?' he demanded roughly. 'Tell me what you have to say and be off with you!'

'Gladly, Sire,' replied the old man confidently, 'but if I were you, I should show a little gratitude to a man who has come to warn you. You are happy today, are you not? You think that you are safe because your sister will soon leave for her husband's home far away. Beware! Beware! You have wronged many people, and your own sister's eighth child will kill you before you are as old as I am.' With that, the man bowed low and hobbled away.

At first Kans was astonished. Then he became frightened and angry. He was so wild with rage and fear that by the time he reached the palace again, he wanted to kill Devaki at once. The wedding guests began to leave. They were frightened at seeing Kans in such a terrible temper. Soon all but Vasudev's closest relatives had left, and even they were ordered out of the palace by Kans. When only Vasudev and Devaki remained, Kans unsheathed his talwaar, a mighty curved sword.

'You must die, Devaki,' he growled. 'A wise man has said that your eighth child will kill me, so I cannot let you live.'

When Vasudev heard this, he was so horrified that he threw himself at Kans' feet in despair.

'How can you believe the words of a strange, wandering beggar?' he cried. 'Please, I beg you, spare Devaki's life. It is not Devaki that you have been warned against, but her child. I promise on my life that I shall hand you all our children as soon as they are born, if only you let Devaki live.'

Even Kans could see that a new-born baby could not kill a grown man. He felt that he could trust Vasudev to keep his word, so he agreed to let Devaki live. However to make sure that they kept their promise, he decided to lock them both up in a prison cell in the palace. He posted guards outside the cell day and night, and Devaki and her husband began their life together in a small bare room, under lock and key.

As the years went by, Devaki and Vasudev grew to love each other more and more dearly, and each child that they lost to Kans made them more determined to save the next. By the time that their seventh child was about to be born, they had learnt that the only way to save their baby was to keep it quiet and try to hide it. Soon a baby girl was born to Devaki, but although they tried to hush her cries, one of the guards heard the child crying and ran to tell the King. Kans hurried to the cell as soon as he was told about the baby. He had come to kill the child with his own hands as he had done all the others. Devaki cried and pleaded with her brother.

'How can this little babe hurt you, my brother?' she wept.

Kans roared angrily as he grabbed the infant from his sister's arms and threw her on to the stone floor. The baby glowed strangely as she fell, and when she hit the ground, she turned into a bolt of lightening which shot up towards heaven.

'You have too much blood on your hands to save you now, evil Kans,' she cried. 'Beware my brother, who will be born to destroy you!'

Devaki and Vasudev were as astonished as Kans and the guards, but if they expected mercy they received none. Kans became even more determined that the eighth child should not be left alive. He doubled the guards at the prison door, arming them with swords and daggers, and he called a sorcerer to protect him with magic spells and potions. Devaki and Vasudev were as determined to protect their child as Kans was to slay it, and for the next year they prayed desperately every day.

The hot weather came and went, and clouds began gathering in the sky, growing heavier with moisture every day until soon they would pour rain on to the hot, dry land. People all over India were praying for the rains to come soon, because without the rain their crops would fail and they would starve.

Krishna, Devaki's eighth child was born as the monsoon rains broke on a very stormy night. A thunderstorm was raging outside, lashing rain against the palace walls. The wind moaned and howled, blowing trees back, and Yamuna River became an angry soaring torrent. All across the kingdom people tried to shelter from the storm wherever they could, and within the palace, the royal nannies, the ayahs, were busy trying to comfort frightened, crying children. All the rest, servants, sentries and courtiers were peering through the windows into the darkness, wondering at this sign of heavenly anger.

As Krishna was born, there was a sharp crack of thunder and a voice boomed across the skies.

'Vasudev, you must take this baby across the river to Gokul and exchange him for your sister's new-born girl. Never fear, your son will be saved. God is with you!'

Devaki and Vasudev realised at once that their prayers had been answered. But what if everyone else had heard the heavenly voice too?' They were sure that Kans and his guards would try to stop Vasudev escaping with the baby. But when they looked around, they were amazed to see that the guards had dropped into a deep sleep exactly where they were standing, and the cell door had magically flown open. Devaki was heartbroken at the thought of losing this child too, so soon after his birth. She held him closely for a few moments, stroking his curly black hair. This child, unlike all her other babies was unusually dark-skinned, looking almost blue at times.

However, it was time for Vasudev to leave, and Devaki watched tearfully as he wrapped the baby Krishna into whatever rags he could find. He put the little bundle into a basket and ran out of the prison and through the palace. No one stopped him, for every man, woman and child in the palace was mysteriously asleep. Vasudev didn't stop to wonder at this sight and hurried towards the Yamuna River, hoping against hope that the ferryman had at least left his boat by the river bank.

It was only when he reached the river that he realised what a foolish hope it was. Even if a boat had been left out that night, it would have been smashed up and carried away by the fierce current. Vasudev decided that his only hope was to swim across the river . He looked up at the angry, crackling sky and called out as loudly as he could, 'I am in your hands, my Lord!'

He stepped into the foaming water, and as he did so, it parted to make a path across to the other side. The many-headed Shesha Nag, the Serpent

King who lived in the river, reared up out of the water with its hood open over Krishna as if sheltering him from the storm. At first Vasudev thought that the snake was about to attack them, but he then realised that it was actually protecting Krishna.

Vasudev reached the other bank safely. It was still raining heavily, but he hurried to the village of Gokul where his sister Yashoda lived. Surprisingly the door to her house was unlocked, and as Vasudev entered he saw that Yashoda and her husband Nand were both fast asleep with their daughter beside them. He crept up quietly, exchanged the babies, and quickly made his way back to the river with the baby girl.

It had stopped raining and the flood waters had subsided by the time Vasudev reached the river. He was able to swim across safely, pushing the baby in her basket in front of him as he swam. It was almost morning by the time Vasudev reached the palace in Mathura, and he was frightened that the guards would awake and find him gone. He need not have worried because everyone in the palace, except Devaki, was still fast asleep when he reached the prison cell. The moment Vasudev was inside however, the locks clanged shut on the cell door. The noise woke the baby, and it started crying as new babies do.

The guards were stirring and the sounds of the usual hustle and bustle soon began to fill the palace. Kans had been waiting anxiously for news of the new baby and ran to the prison cell as soon as he was told of the child's cries. Devaki was holding the baby in her arms, cuddling and soothing her. She began to cry when she saw Kans, pleading for mercy. Kans ignored her pleas. He tore the baby away from his sister and was about to smash her to the ground, when the infant flew out of his arms.

'Kans, you wicked child-killer!' cried the baby. 'He who will destroy you is already born. God commands you to release Devaki and her husband, for you have nothing more to fear from them!' With that, the child vanished before their eyes.

Kans was beside himself at being so easily tricked, and he threatened to kill Vasudev and Devaki at once. However, the guards and all the courtiers who heard what had happened realised that such an act would surely bring disaster upon them all. They begged Kans to spare his sister and her husband, reminding him that this was God's command. Kans finally agreed to let Devaki and Vasudev live, but he refused to set them free. He was so angry at being deceived, and so frightened for his own life, that he vowed to kill every baby boy in Mathura.

'I shall not rest until I have found and killed this horrible child!' he thundered.

Immediately, he ordered his soldiers to search all the houses in Mathura, and to kill every baby boy they found. Soon, mothers throughout the kingdom were in a panic trying to save their babies and their little boys from the soldiers. Kans did not rest until the only children left in Mathura were girls, and for days, all that could be heard in the kingdom were the cries of screaming children and weeping mothers.

If Krishna had been in Mathura he would surely have been killed, but for a while at least, he was safe. What Kans did not know was that the child he feared was being raised as the son of Nand and Yashoda in Gokul, which lay outside his kingdom.

Diksha Dalal-Clayton

Janmashtami

Soon it will be midnight.
Janmashtami will be here.
Bring out Krishna's statue.
Hear the people cheer.

Vijay! Vijay!
Salute the victory!

Celebrate the hour
He began his life on earth.
Honour the day
Of baby Krishna's birth.

Vijay! Vijay!
Salute the victory!

John Foster

GANESH CHATURTHI

Ganesh Chaturthi celebrates the birth of Ganesh or Ganpati and takes place on the fourth day of the Hindu month, Bradrapad, which falls sometime in August or September.

Many Hindus pray to Ganesh – a form of God depicted as having an elephant head and the body of a man. Ganesh is thought of as the remover of obstacles and as the god of wisdom.

In the time leading up to the festival local crafts-makers are busy making clay figures of Ganesh for people to buy. On Ganesh Chaturthi a family will bring their figure into the house. It is then kept for one and a half, five, seven or ten days according to family custom, during which time special prayers are said morning and night and offerings of coconut are made. At the end of this period the figure is immersed in the sea, river or a well to cries of 'Ganpati Bappa Moraya, Pudhachya Varshi Lavakanya' (Oh Lord Ganesh, come soon next year).

Why Ganesh has an elephant's head

The goddess Parvati longed for a child. Her husband, Lord Shiva, left her on her own for long periods of time and she often felt very lonely. 'Oh, my lord, how I wish for a child,' she would say.

One morning while taking her daily bath Parvati collected all the skin rubbed from her body and moulded it into the shape of a baby boy. Then she breathed life into the figure and was overjoyed when it began to move. Parvati called her son Ganesh.

Ganesh would stand guarding the gate while his mother bathed and he took his duties as a guard very seriously. All went well for a while but then one day Lord Shiva returned home and demanded to be allowed in. Now, not knowing his father, Ganesh tried to stop him from entering which of course made Lord Shiva very angry, so angry that he struck Ganesh's head clean off his body.

Poor Parvati was heart-broken when she discovered what had happened. 'You've killed my child,' she sobbed. Lord Shiva knew he had to do something.

'Don't grieve,' he said to his wife, 'I will put things right.' And he set off to find a new head for Ganesh. He decided that he would take the head from the first animal he found that faced north.

Soon he saw a huge elephant; it was in fact the god Indra's elephant. But being a great hunter with a promise to keep, Lord Shiva cut off the elephant's head, carried it back to the palace and put it on Ganesh's body. Parvati was so happy to have her child alive again; she loved his new shape and she thought he was a very special child. Indeed, Ganesh was so special he became a friend and god to the Hindu people.

Renuka Singh

Ganesha Chaturthi

Wash him in the river
wash him in the sea –
let him bring good fortune
merrily to me!
Because it is his birthday,
a-learning I must go:
Ganesha Chaturthi
likes it to be so.

Learning in the morning
and in the afternoon –
I'll shade my eyes and turn away –
I won't look at the moon!

Wash him, when the music
and dancing all is done.
Dip him in the ocean...
A Festival's fun!

Jean Kenward

A prayer at Ganesha Chaturthi

O Great Ganesha
Most wise most venerable,
Bringer of good luck,
Bless my son, my little Ravi
On his first day at school.
Give him joy in his studies
And grant him good fortune,
All praise, Great Ganesha,
All praise on your birthday.

Theresa Heine

Ganesh's broken tusk

If there was one thing that Ganesh loved to do it was to eat, and best of all he loved sweet things like fruits, cakes and puddings. One night after feasting on all his favourite foods Ganesh went out riding on his vehicle, the rat. The big round moon lit the countryside around them. All of a sudden a large snake slithered across the path in front of the rat, frightening him so much that he stopped dead in his tracks sending Ganesh flying. As he hit the ground Ganesh's enormous stomach burst open and all his supper came tumbling out on to the ground.

Ganesh picked himself up and, pulling the gaping hole in his stomach together, he seized the snake and tied it around his middle to hold his stomach fast. Then Ganesh heard laughter; but who could be laughing at his misfortune? He looked around but could see no one. So he looked up and there was Lord Chandra, the moon, laughing and laughing. Ganesh was furious. 'How dare you laugh at me?' he shouted and, breaking off one of his tusks, he hurled it as hard as he could at the moon, cursing Lord Chandra as he did so and saying that all who looked at him would hear bad things about themselves.

The story goes that people shunned Lord Chandra, who felt so ashamed he hid himself in a lotus flower. Then there was no moonlight in the world and the gods begged Ganesh to lift the curse; Lord Chandra, too, begged for forgiveness. So Ganesh removed the curse but said that Chandra's insolence should always be remembered.

'Whoever sees the moon on my birthday shall suffer the effects of the curse,' he said.

So now it is considered to be unlucky to look at the moon on Ganesh Chaturthi.

Renuka Singh

HARVEST

People's sense of being part of the natural world goes back to earliest times and giving thanks for harvest has been something human beings have done ever since they first farmed land, for it has its roots in the basis of human survival.

Harvest celebrations in Great Britain date back to pre-Christian times and are believed to have their origins in mankind's need to revere the life-giving spirit thought to live in ripened crops. The success of harvest governed the lives of people and their domestic animals and as far back as Saxon times farmers offered the first sheaf of corn they cut to one of the fertility gods to safeguard a good harvest the next year. In medieval times the last sheaf cut – the Harvest 'dolly' – was thought to house the spirit of the corn. So the 'Corn Dolly' or Harvest Queen was made from this and after honouring it at harvest supper it was kept – often tied to the rafters in the farmhouse – until the following year when it was either ploughed back into the field or burned. However, it was not until the 1840s that the tradition of September harvest thanksgiving services in churches began. For Christian people now, harvest thanksgiving is a celebration of God, the creator, and of mankind's continuation of the creative cycle.

There are many other celebrations of harvest all over the world by different faith communities and at different times of year. These include the following.

Onam. This is celebrated in every Hindu home in Kerala, South India, in the mouth of Chingam (August/September) marking the Malayalam harvest season and the first harvest of the year. Preparations start ten days before the festival when homes are decorated with Atthappoo or Onathappan, a ten-tier design of flowers, a layer being built for each day. On the day of Onam people bathe early and put on new clothes. Lunch time is a special meal eaten at home after which there is dancing and in some places, such as Cochin, famous snake-boat races are held in long snake-like boats called chundans.

Pongal. Observed on the first day of the Tamil month of Thai (mid-January) this marks the end of the harvest season in Tamil Nadu, South India. A good harvest of sugar cane and rice ensures a time of plenty and prosperity. 'Pongal' is actually a word for a mixture of rice, milk, moong dal and jaggery or sugar and is derived from 'Ponga' meaning to boil: the pot containing the mixture has to boil over to symbolise plenty and prosperity. The festival lasts four days: on the first homes are cleaned, bonfires lit to burn anything useless, kolam designs are made in front of doorways and homes decorated with plaited coconut and mango leaves. The Pongal dish is cooked on the second day of the festival.

Thai Harvest. In some regions of Ayutthaya, Thailand, a festival is celebrated in honour of the rice goddess. Boiled cakes (red and white in colour) wrapped in banana leaves are taken to the paddy fields and offered to the goddess. Rice is also scattered on the ground for animals and birds to eat.

Yam Harvest of West Africa. This is celebrated in August or September and its origins lie in the offering of a portion of the new crop to the 'god of the yam' who was thought to be responsible for its growth. Sacrifices are made to the god of the land to encourage good harvests in the future: shrines of the yam gods are given a coat of paint and offerings of yam are made. Sometimes dances are performed and the dancers wear beautifully decorated masks.

Moon Festival. Chinese people celebrate the Moon Festival on the fifteenth day of the eighth lunar month (September) when the brightest full moon occurs. Prayers are offered to the moon for good rice harvest, rice wine is drunk and special 'moon cakes' are baked and eaten. Lanterns are an important part of the festival and when darkness falls incense sticks are burned and a lantern procession greets the bright moon.

Baisakhi. This Sikh spring festival (see page 83) is in part a celebration of the Punjabi spring wheat harvest. In some parts of India the Hindu festival of Diwali is also a harvest celebration (see page 141).

Sukkot. Also known as the Feast of Tabernacles, Sukkot is the time when Jewish people celebrate thanksgiving, from 15th to 22nd day of Tishri (usually October). The festival recalls the period of almost forty years when God protected the Israelites in the wilderness, after they had left Egypt and before they reached the Promised Land. During this time they lived in temporary dwellings, called sukkah, and today Jewish families erect a small hut or sukkah to remind them of this. The roof of a sukkah is made of plant material – leaves and branches cut for the purpose – and sufficient space is left in the roof for the sky and stars to be seen through it. The sukkah is decorated inside with fruits, leaves and bottles of water or oil; meals are eaten here during the festival. During Sukkot four symbols are used to make blessings to God. These are sometimes called the Four Species and are branches of palm, called Lulav; leaves or myrtle, called Hadas; willow, called Arava; and the fruit of a citron (similar to a lemon), called Etrog. Sukkot also celebrates the Earth's bounty and in some places is a grape and fruit harvest.

Nduku's dream

In Kenya children are expected to work in the fields and at home after school.

Nduku and her friends had to tend the maize and beans. They helped to plant the seeds at the beginning of the rainy season and they were growing well. But so were the weeds!

The children weeded between the seedlings. As they worked, they sang about *harambee*.

Harambee is the national motto in Kenya. It is a Kiswahili word which means 'pull together'.

As she worked, Nduku thought about the hard times in previous years when there was drought. This year things were better. The harvest would be good.

But there was still one big problem. When the people gathered in the harvest the merchants would not pay a fair price for the crops. Nduku wished they could get paid more. She wished her family could live without struggling all the time.

She thought of her mother who was expecting a new baby. Nduku hoped it would be a girl. It wasn't that she didn't like boys, but she already had three brothers and dearly wished for a sister. She began to daydream about the new baby. What sort of life would it have? Would it grow up in a better world, a world of hope and justice?

'Nduku!' called Roda, one of her friends. 'What are you dreaming about today?'

'I was thinking of the future,' said Nduku.

'My mother says the future is in the hands of the women,' said Roda. Both their mothers were members of the village women's group. Nduku's mother was one of the leaders.

'They've been meeting today,' said Nduku. 'Let's go and see if there's any news.'

Off they went. There *was* news – good news. The women's group had found a way to get a better price for the harvest. If all the farmers in the village put their crops together into what they called a 'cereal bank', they could sell the whole lot together and the merchants would have to pay a fair price or get no crops at all.

Everyone in the village was delighted with the idea. When harvest time came everyone worked together. Nduku and her friends helped pick the plump, ripe maize and carry it in baskets to the cereal bank.

The women's idea was a great success and the farmers got a fair price. Everyone was very happy and they decided to have a great celebration. There was drumming, dancing and singing. Nduku and Roda joined in enthusiastically.

After a while, Nduku sat down to watch. She began to dream again. She thought of the women's group. It was a good example of *harambee* – pulling together – and she felt proud. The women of the village had used some of the money to make new school uniforms for the children. Nduku decided that when she grew up she would join the women's group. Perhaps she would even become a leader.

As she wondered a voice interrupted her thoughts. 'Nduku, Nduku!' It was Roda again. 'Your mother wants you to come home.'

'But why?' said Nduku. 'The celebration's not finished.'

'She wants you to see your new baby. You have a baby sister!'

'A sister!' cried Nduku. 'That's great news.' She jumped up and ran home thinking, 'Dreams can come true.'

Anonymous

A present for harvest

Everybody thought that Mr Goss's classroom looked like a greengrocer's shop. This was because it was harvest time and the children were bringing fruit and vegetables for their harvest festival. Mr Goss said that everyone must bring something, even if it was only one potato or one carrot, but most of the children brought more than that. Paul brought a bag of apples, Yasmin brought some tomatoes, and Razwan brought a big bag of grapes from his father's shop.

Mr Goss said that after the harvest assembly, all the food would be put into boxes, and taken round to the old people who lived near the school. He told the children that if they knew of any grandmas or grandpas who lived alone and would like a box of food, they should tell him and he would put that person's name on his list.

Most of the children were puzzled. All their grandmas and grandpas lived with their own families. Mr Goss said that they were lucky – but he knew a lot of old people who didn't have a family to look after them.

'Many of them,' he said, 'don't have enough money to buy food or to keep themselves warm.'

On the morning of the harvest assembly, all the fruit and vegetables and jars of jam and tins of baked beans were arranged on tables at one end of the hall. The school cook had made a big piece of bread in the shape of a bundle of wheat, and in among the stalks of the wheat were lots of little bread mice, all shiny and golden. Mr Goss said they were harvest mice.

Some of the smallest children had baskets with apples and bananas and oranges in them, and they came out to the front while the others were singing their harvest song, and held their baskets up so that everyone could see. Then Mrs Grant told them about children all over the world who didn't have enough to eat, and about what everyone could do to try and help them. She said that after dinner, when all the food had been sorted out and put into boxes, a few teachers and some children would take them round to the old people.

When they got back to their classroom, Mr Goss noticed the children whispering in a corner.

'What's the matter?' he asked.

No one wanted to say, but then Parveen said, 'Changis and Najma saw two deaders when they were coming to school!'

Everyone stopped what they were doing and stared at Changis and Najma.

'What do you mean?' asked Mr Goss. 'Do you mean someone is dead?'

'Yes – two deaders. We saw them,' said Changis.

Mr Goss went and sat at his desk. 'Come over here, you two, and tell me what you saw. Was it a car accident? Was somebody knocked down in the road?'

Najma shook her head. 'No,' she said, 'they're in a house.'

Mr Goss didn't know what to think. 'If they're in a house,' he said, 'I think perhaps they were asleep.'

'No,' said Changis. 'We shouted and they didn't move. And a big boy threw a stone.'

Mr Goss decided that he would go and have a look. 'But if you are making all this up,' he told the children, 'I shall be very, very angry.'

Mr Goss found someone to look after his class, then he and Changis and Najma set off up the road. The children lived next door to each other in a road near the park, and always went to and from school together. Some of the houses in the streets nearby were going to be pulled down to make room for some new flats, and there were planks nailed across the doors and windows. The little front gardens were full of tall weeds and thistles, and there was rubbish everywhere.

'That's the house!' cried Changis suddenly, pointing. 'The one near the tree.'

As they came up to the house, Mr Goss said, 'But it's all boarded up – how could you see anything inside?' And then he understood.

Behind the straggly privet hedge in the front garden was an old mattress that somebody had thrown out. And on the mattress lay a very old man and a very old lady. They were fast asleep – Mr Goss could see them

breathing – and they had piled all their things on top of them to keep themselves warm, newspaper, old coats and shoes, boxes and boots and carrier bags, and big old quilt which must have been thrown out with the mattress.

'They're not dead!' said Mr Goss. 'They're asleep. Look at them breathing.'

'They were dead when we saw them,' said Changis.

As he spoke, there was a movement at the bottom of the pile. The old man opened his eyes and tried to sit up. He looked very angry and the children ran and hid behind Mr Goss.

For a long while the old man stared at Mr Goss, screwing up his little red eyes against the sunlight. Then he said in a scratchy voice, 'You got a fag?'

'Er – I'm afraid not. I don't smoke. But – ' Mr Goss felt in his pocket and brought out two £1 coins. 'Here – get yourselves something to eat – there's a café just down the road.'

The old man got to his feet and took the money. He didn't say 'Thank you'. He just nodded to Mr Goss, and shook the old lady, who woke up and began to complain. Together they started to collect their things, stuffing the papers and shoes into carrier bags, wrapping themselves in the coats.

Suddenly Najma said, 'You're a grandma and a grandpa – you can have a box of food! We'll bring it after dinner.'

'I don't think they'll be here after dinner, Najma,' said Mr Goss. 'I think they're getting ready to go.'

'But they'll come back after dinner,' said Najma, 'and you said if we knew about a grandma and a grandpa who wanted a box of food....'

'Very well,' said Mr Goss. 'You're quite right, Najma. We'll come back after dinner.'

When they got back to school, Changis and Najma helped to fill a box for the old man and the old lady. Mr Goss said that it would be best to give them things that did not need to be cooked, because he thought that perhaps the grandma might not have a stove to cook on. So the children put in apples and grapes and biscuits, a packet of margarine and a jar of jam, and, for a treat, two of the cook's shiny bread mice.

'It's for our own grandma and grandpa,' Najma said.

After dinner, the children went back to the house with Mr Goss. There was no sign of the two old people. Everything had gone except the mattress.

'They might come back tonight,' said Changis. He looked very sad. 'Can we leave the box for them?'

They put the box under a corner of the mattress, so that even if it rained it would not get wet, and went back to school.

The next morning the two children came running into the classroom.

'They came back! They came back!' they told Mr Goss.

'How do you know?' asked Mr Goss. 'Did you see them?'

'No – but all the things have gone – the box is empty! Do you think they were happy to have the food?'

'I hope they were,' said Mr Goss. 'I hope they had a very happy harvest.'

Nadya Smith

Harvest song

Debbie Campbell

Intro:

1. Ev - ery-where we go   Trees and flow-ers grow.   Nat - ture's boun - ti - ful ri - vers o - ver-flow,   Gi - ving us a   green and pleas - ant land, A friend___ on   whom we can___ de - pend.

Chorus: slower

Lend a hand___ to the peo - ple___   in need.

We have plen-ty to feed____ The peo-ple in need.

2. Everyone we meet
Is watching what they eat.
Counting the calories
Jogging down the street.
Living where there's food enough to share
It's only fair we ought to care.

Chorus
Spare a thought for the people in need
We have plenty to feed
The people in need.

3. People far away
Waiting every day
Watching their forests and rivers waste away
Dying on the dry dusty sand
Where once was green and pleasant land.

Chorus
Lend a hand to the people in need
We have plenty to feed
The people in need.

from 'Thanksgiving'

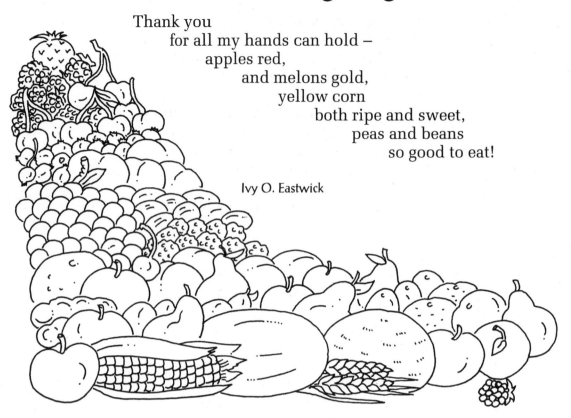

Thank you
    for all my hands can hold –
      apples red,
        and melons gold,
          yellow corn
            both ripe and sweet,
              peas and beans
                so good to eat!

Ivy O. Eastwick

Harvest home

Wheat is all cut,
Oats safe in bags,
Barley just ripe,
Tractor zig-zags
Bumping downhill
Trailer with beans
And at the wheel
Girl in blue jeans,
In orchard below,
Baskets of plums
Wait under trees
Till fruit lorry comes.
Harvest is in.
And home go the growers,
The pickers, the mowers;
Let dancing begin
At the end of day
Now harvest is in.

Leonard Clark

Harvest home

The boughs do shake and the bells do ring.
So merrily comes our harvest in,
Our harvest in, our harvest in,
So merrily comes our harvest in.

We have ploughed and we have sowed,
We have reaped and we have mowed,
We have brought home every load,
We've got our harvest in.

Hip, hip, hip, harvest home.

Anonymous

Corn dolly

'Tis but a thing of straw, they say,
Yet even straw can sturdy be
Plaited into a doll like me.
And in the days of long ago
To help the seeds once more to grow
I was an offering to the gods.
A very simple way indeed
Of asking them to intercede
That barn and granary o'erflow
At harvest time, with fruit and corn
To fill again Amalthea's horn.

Anonymous

Thanksgiving time

When all the leaves are off the boughs,
And nuts and apples gathered in,
And cornstalks waiting for the cows,
And pumpkins safe in barn and bin;

The Mother says, 'My children dear,
The fields are brown, and Autumn flies;
Thanksgiving Day is very near,
And we must make Thanksgiving pies.'

Anonymous

The harvest beat

Reach up high, stand on your toes,
Pluck the fruit which on the branch grows.
Reach for the apple, reach for the pear,
Over here and over there.

Now bend down and look around,
Gather vegetables from the ground.
Pull the carrots, bend your knees,
Pluck tomatoes, beans and peas.

Pick the grapes which grow on the vine,
Plump and juicy with sunshine.
Drop them in the bucket, stamp your feet,
Make grape juice with the harvest beat!

Do a somersault frontwards and back,
Lift that bale and carry that sack.
Swing that scythe from side to side,
Bounce up and down on the haywagon ride.

Stretch to your left, stretch to your right.
Harvest this food in the Autumn sunlight.
Twist and turn, kick up your heels,
Clap your hands and dance your reels!

Anonymous

An American Indian prayer

Oh, Mother of Man
Oh, Sun Father
Oh, Corn Mother
Thank you for your gifts.
The understanding of colour
The understanding of music
The understanding of clouds
The understanding of work.
It is then we teach our children
It is then we acquire laughter
It is then we acquire a smile
And the soul is healed.
Thank you for this
understanding
Oh, Mother of Man
Oh, Sun Father
Oh, Corn Mother.

Charles Loloma

Elleni and the sharing bread

The story goes that once upon a time, at the foot of a great mountain, there were two villages, one on each side of the river. The people of each village hated the other with a great hatred. No boats crossed the water that rushed between them. And if the other village was mentioned at all, it was with a curse.

Elleni, youngest daughter of the village chief Allarik, could not understand why.

'How did the hatred begin?' she asked.

'More questions!' said her father. 'It has always been so, and it will always be so.'

And her mother said, 'Be grateful that you live in *this* village, Elleni.'

She asked her older sister and brothers as she helped to bring in the wheat in the fields under the mountain.

'Oh it was a quarrel,' said one. 'Two brothers quarrelled, so I heard. One took his family to live across the other side. Long time ago now.'

'They stole grain in the night!' said another. 'That's how it started. Of course, we do have the best wheat fields this side.'

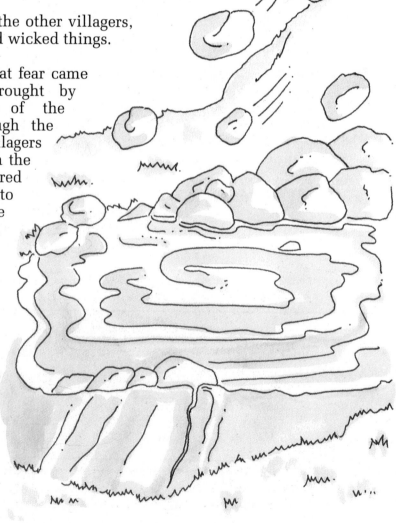

'Oh, they are a bad lot, the other villagers, Elleni. They do strange and wicked things. Forget about them.'

It was that year that great fear came down the Mountain, brought by Brendik, the youngest of the shepherds. He ran through the fields, shouting to the villagers who were now bringing in the last of the wheat. He staggered into the village. Straight to the Hall of Meetings he went and hammered loudly on the summoning bell. As soon as Allarik and the others began to crowd in, he blurted out:

'There is danger. You must move out of the village!'

'What do you mean? What's happened?' Allarik demanded.

'In the night,' said the young shepherd, 'there was a terrible noise like thunder. Stones, boulders, came rushing down the mountainside and

blocked the river that flows into our river. A deep lake is building up, crashing against the rocks. Soon it will all come bursting down. We must move out now. The water is pushing all along the stones. Look. It could break through the east side of the ridge and come straight down on us. Or....'

'Well, go on,' cried the villagers.

'Or if it breaks through the western ridge, well, it will fall on the other village.'

A grim smile came for a moment on Allarik's face. Then he turned to the villagers.

'Come, everyone! There is no time to lose. Pack your belongings – everything you value. We must climb to the South Hill. We'll camp there until the mountain decides between us.'

In the turmoil, Elleni had a question for her father:

'But shouldn't we send a message to the other village, to warn them too?'

'Are you mad, girl?' Allarik shouted. 'Let them see to themselves. Help your mother and sisters pack the food!' He laughed angrily. 'Warn the other village? What next!'

That night on the South Hill the campfire flickered on stern faces as the villagers sat still, praying and listening. As the sun rose their eyes searched the area beneath the mountain. Now they could see the high wall of boulders. Their eyes grew wide with fear at the thought of the water building up behind it. For three days they waited. Then, on the third day, just after dawn, it came. With a crashing roar the torrent of rock and flood burst open and down towards the ridge before them. At first the ridge held firm. Then, as the water and rock continued to pound, it began to shift. It was going to give – but which side would give, which side? In a few seconds they knew. Let there be praise! It was the west side, the part furthest away from them, that began to crumble. With a deafening roar, the torrent burst through in its angry rush – straight down to the other village.

Laughing and singing, the villagers on South Hill gathered their belongings, dismantled their makeshift shelters, stamped out the fires and ran to their safe homes. As they passed the Hall of Meetings, Allarik called out, 'Finish bringing in the wheat. Return here this afternoon. We'll have the Sharing Bread, and we'll sacrifice to the Mountain. Then we'll have our harvest feast!'

At home, Elleni's mother bustled into the kitchen.

'Elleni, girl, I've not heard that corn-stone grind these last ten minutes. Don't sit gazing ahead, doing nothing.'

'Mother,' Elleni asked, 'those people in the other village. What has happened to them?

Her mother stopped for a moment and sighed. Yes, she thought, what has happened to them? Then she turned angrily.

'Think what will happen to you, girl, if that flour is not ready. It's your turn to bring the corn for the Sharing Bread. It's your turn to present thebread in the Place of Meetings this afternoon. Will you bring disgrace on your father's house?'

Elleni pulled the great stone round, crushing the grains of wheat. The first of the flour trickled through onto the ground.

The Place of Meetings was full. No one could remember the tables being piled so high with food. There would be so much to enjoy: eating, drinking, dancing far into the night.

Now Allarik called for silence.

'Let us give praise and thanks for our safety and for our harvest,' he said. The mountain has saved us and our village, and...' he paused. In his mind again, and into the minds of the villagers, now that the busy preparations were done, came thoughts of the other village. Allarik shook himself, and spoke again. 'The Sharing Bread,' he said abruptly, turning to Elleni. She brought forward the large, flat, round loaf.

Allarik reminded them: 'Each family will break off a piece, and each member will share it. But take one piece back with you tonight to place beneath your hearth stone, so that good fortune will be with you throughout the coming year.'

Again he stopped. All had heard the noise. Someone was outside. There was a scuttling of stones, a dragging of feet, and a heavy groaning. Then into the open doorway stepped a terrible figure – a man, exhausted, wild-eyed. His rags clung wetly to his bruised body. He staggered against the door post and would have fallen. But he took hold of himself and came up to Allarik.

'Please help us. We have nothing, nothing. Our houses are gone. Many are dead, others trapped in the ruins, children screaming for their parents. Even the living will soon die if we don't get food – and you have – his eyes gazed at the tables – you have all this.'

The villagers had pushed back against the walls, staring. He was from the other village!

'I swam across the river,' he said. 'You must help us.' He held out his hands and slowly turned around, looking pleadingly at them all. No one spoke or moved.

In the silence, he turned back to Allarik, disbelief in his eyes. Was no one going to help? Then it was that Elleni, still holding the Sharing Bread, went up to him. She broke off a piece of bread, and put it into his hand.

A sigh of agreement went through the Place of Meetings. Allarik stepped forward and put his arm round Elleni.

'Oh, my people, we are in great shame for the terrible things we have done. It has taken a child to show us what we buried in our hearts.' He grasped the other villager's hand which still had in it a piece of Sharing Bread. 'We have done you a great wrong,' he said. 'Forgive us all.' He turned to the villagers.

'There will be no feast until the other village is fed.' He held up the Bread. 'Let none share this who does not also share this promise.'

Taking the food from the tables, the villagers sped to their houses for more. They rushed down to the river bank, and into their boats, to cross over to the other village....

Arthur Scholey

Sukkot

Myrtle, palm and willow;
willow, myrtle, palm.

Wave your branches to the earth,
raise them to the sun.

Myrtle, palm and willow;
willow, myrtle, palm.

Stretch your branches north and west,
curl them up and down.

Myrtle, palm and willow;
willow, myrtle, palm.

Spread your branches south and east,
swing them all around.

Myrtle, palm and willow;
willow, myrtle, palm.

Swing your branches to the earth,
wave them all around;
show that God is everywhere,
raise them to the sun!

Myrtle, palm and willow;
willow, myrtle, palm.

Judith Nicholls

I'm building a sukkah

Traditional Jewish

1. I'm build-ing a suk-kah, my ham-mer does-n't stop,

La-di-da bim bam bi-ri bi-ri bam. Oh bring me the schach for I've

reached the ve-ry top! La-di-da bim bam bi-ri bi-ri bam.

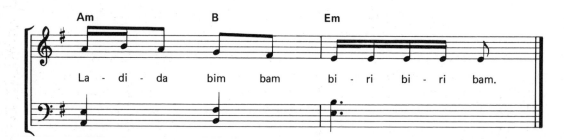

La-di-da bim bam bi-ri bi-ri bam.

2. I'll sit in the sukkah like Noah in the Ark,
La-di-da, etc.
I'll drink and be merry from morning to dark!
La-di-da, etc.

3. Come friends and neighbours, come right along,
La-di-da, etc.
Join us in eating and singing a song,
La-di-da, etc.

ROSH HASHANAH

Rosh Hashanah, the Jewish New Year, is celebrated on the first day of the month of Tishri; traditionally it is the anniversary of the creation of the world (the date from which the Jewish calendar is reckoned). The festival falls in September and is celebrated over two days; these and the following eight days lead up to the festival of Yom Kippur, the Day of Atonement.

For Jewish people, Rosh Hashanah is a solemn occasion, a time to think back over one's life and behaviour during the past year and to ask for God's forgiveness. The focus of the festival is the service which takes place in the synagogue; the shofar (ram's horn) is blown to call everyone to pray for forgiveness and to recall the birth of Abraham's son, Isaac, and the sacrifice of the ram by Abraham.

Apples dipped in honey are eaten for a good and sweet new year. Other festive foods include honey cake, a sweet noodle pudding, Tagelach (cake in honey) and Tzimmis (carrots with honey). Many people send new year cards and the traditional greeting is 'May you be written and sealed for a good year'.

Rosh Hashanah

There was a sound so sweet and clear
It said to me, 'The New Year's here.'

It said, 'Remember to be brave.'
It said, 'Remember to be good.'

And when I heard the shofar's call
I stood up straight and said I would.

Ben Aronin

For a good and sweet new year

Bees, bees,
Give us your honey!
Give us your honey, please.
We have special round bread,
Apples, too, round and red,
That came from the orchard trees.
We'll eat them with honey,
All golden and sunny,
When Rosh Hashanah is here;
Honey, apples, and bread
When the blessing is said
For a good and sweet New Year.

Sadie Rose Weilerstein

Rosh Hashannah

(Kiddush is a prayer: 'May God in his goodness grant us a sweet year.')
The candles tremble on our faces,
In the evening the cloth is spread,
All the family take their places,
For the Kiddush has now been said.

May God in his goodness,
A sweet year grant us,
Is the prayer we have in mind,
As we dip apple slices into the honey,
We hope all our sins we've left behind.

Janet E. Greenyer

Tapuchim ud' vash (Apples and honey)

Traditional Jewish

DIWALI

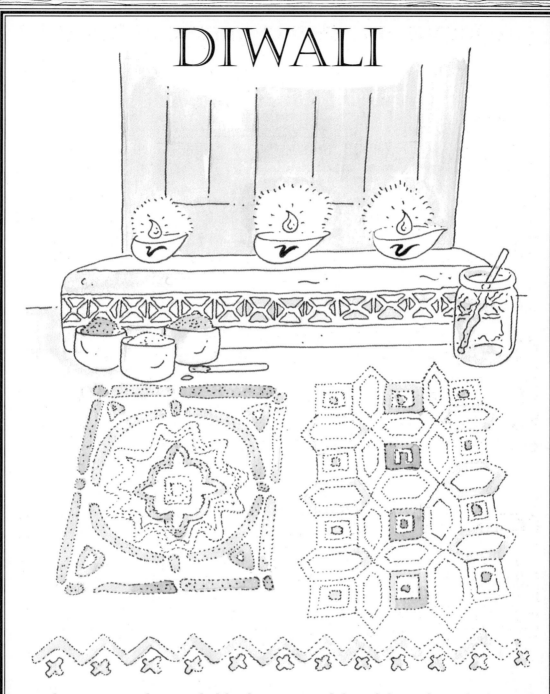

Diwali or Deepavali is probably the most widely celebrated Hindu festival in India. Diwali day itself falls on the 15th day (amavasya) of the month of Kartik according to the Hindu calendar (October–November), the day of no moon when the night is pitch black, though the festival is celebrated over five days starting on the 13th day of Kartik. The word Diwali comes from Deepavali which means 'a row of lights'.

A few days before the festival starts people clean their homes thoroughly and rooms are often whitewashed or painted, so Diwali brings cleanliness. Preparations also begin on the festival foods, both sweet and savoury.

The first day of the festival is known as Dhan Teras. Dhan means wealth and Teras means the 13th day. On this day new things – utensils, or sometimes clothes or jewellery – are bought. The second day is called in the north Roop Chandas: Roop means beauty and Chandas is the 14th day of the month. On this day people take a ritual bath and women are said to 'take out their beauty' in preparation for the Lakshmi puja to be performed the next day.

The third day is Diwali which is devoted to Lakshmi, the goddess of wealth and prosperity. Every home is decorated with divas which are put in each and every room, in front of the house and on the walls, even in cow sheds, to welcome Lakshmi who, it is believed, will overlook any home where no divas are lit. Beautiful rangoli or mandana patterns are made in front of homes, in courtyards and in places where the Lakshmi puja is performed. Rangoli is a design made with different coloured powders; mandana is a design made with lime dissolved in water, and red clay dissolved in water. On this day people dress in their best clothes and perform a special puja for Lakshmi. Silver coins may be placed in front of a picture or statue of the goddess and a large diva, which must remain alight for the whole night, is lit during the puja. This burning diva is placed on some grains of rice. Business people keep their shops and offices open for the whole night and also perform puja; they close their yearly accounts and open new account books for the coming year. It is said that Lord Ram, his wife Sita, and Laxman returned from exile on this day. To show their happiness and to welcome the three back home, the people of Ayodhya lit divas and candles throughout the city. (Sita is believed to be an incarnation of Lakshmi which is one reason why Lakshmi came to be worshipped on this day.)

The fourth day of the festivities is known in the north as Govardhana puja. People shape cow dung into mounds in the form of a man and woman in front of their homes, a diva is lit in the morning and puja performed. Govardhana is a small mountain near Mathura which, according to the Puranas, was lifted by Lord Krishna on his little finger to give shelter to the entire population and their cattle from a deluge caused by Indra in anger at their love for the young Krishna. On this day too, Annakoot – the Mountain of Food – is observed and in Nathdwara many different dishes are raised ceremoniously in the form of a mountain before the deity. People visit their friends, relations and neighbours, offering them sweets and many different savouries and wishing them happiness and prosperity. Cards are another popular form of greeting sent at this time.

The final day, the fifth day, is Bhai Duj or Bhaiya Dooj (Bhai means brother). On this day a brother will visit his sister's home for a meal and she will mark a tilak on his forehead, and he will present her with a gift.

Renuka Singh

A Diwali surprise

Sandeep felt sorry for the postman. Every morning he had to climb up the concrete stairs and along the dark stone corridors of their block of flats. Sometimes he had only one letter for their corridor and it was often for the

people who lived at the far end. Sandeep wondered how often the postman had to get new shoes – all that walking must wear out the leather soles.

Every morning was the same. Clomp, clomp along the corridor. Rat-a-tat-tat at a door. Sometimes there was a thud on Sandeep's doormat and the boy would rush to see what the postman had brought.

One Monday in November, it was different. First of all, the postman was much later that usual. Sandeep could hear him stopping more frequently. Clomp, clomp. Rat-a-tat-tat. Clomp, clomp. Rat-a-tat-tat. Sandeep had time to get his front door open, just in case the postman had a letter for his father. 'What made you late?' he asked. The postman held out a handful of mail.

'Just look!' he said. 'It must be everybody's birthday round here. I'm late because there is much more post that usual.'

Sandeep laughed. 'That's because it is our festival,' he said. 'We shall be getting cards from our family in India and from our relations in Harrow. I expect you'll be late all this week.' The postman nodded his head.

'I guessed something was up,' he said. 'You must tell me what the festival is about – only not today; I'm late.' They said goodbye and Sandeep ran into the flat with a pile of cards.

Each day was the same. The postman arrived at the block of flats with a heavier bag and he had to call at nearly every door. On Thursday Sandeep was feeling really sorry for him.

'Mummy,' he said, 'our postman doesn't know anything about Diwali. Could we give him a Diwali surprise tomorrow?' His mother

liked the idea and the two of them spent the afternoon planning how to tell the postman about the festival.

First of all, Sandeep helped his mother to make some coconut barfi, sweets made of evaporated milk, sugar and desiccated coconut. 'When it has set, you can arrange some pieces in a box for the postman to take home to his little girl,' she said. Then she began to plan a rangoli pattern to put on the floor of the corridor just outside their flat. 'I will get up early in the morning and draw it properly,' she said. 'Then it won't get trodden on by all the people coming home from work tonight.'

'What about the divas?' asked Sandeep.

'They are in the drawer under my bed,' replied his mother. 'We will put nightlights in them and you can light them when you hear the postman coming along the corridor.'

Next morning everything was ready. The barfi was in a pretty box, decorated by Sandeep. 'We have sweets at Diwali to remind us of all the good things we share,' he said. Mother had drawn a rangoli pattern for the corridor. Sandeep could see the shape of the lotus flower and some little footprints. 'That means we want goddess Lakshmi to come to our house,' said Sandeep.

Clomp, clomp. Rat-a-tat-tat. 'He's coming!' Sandeep rushed to light the divas. 'Postman! Postman! It's Diwali!' he called. 'Come and see how we enjoy it.' The Postman was thrilled with the box of barfi and he congratulated Mrs Patel on the lovely pattern on their doorstep.

'We wanted to thank you for bringing all those cards,' said Sandeep's mother.

Then Sandeep produced his biggest surprise – a card he had coloured with his felt-tips, a card which said: *Happy Diwali, Postman.*

Dorothy J. Taylor

Divali

Putting oil lamps round the door,
Making patterns on the floor,
Sending cards to all our friends,
Happy that the monsoon ends.

Giving fruit and sticky sweets,
Lighting fireworks in the street.
In the temple we all pray,
Now Divali starts today.

Wendy P. Larmont

Light the diwa

(A diwa is a small oil lamp often lit at Diwali.)
Drive away the darkness
In comes the light.
Worship joyfully
At your home shrine.
Laxmi waits;
Invite her in for blessings.

Chris Riley

The story of Diwali in song

Punitha Perinparaja

Diwali

Ha - nu - man's ___ ar - my ___ helped him.

Return to Chorus

De - mon king was slain, Si - ta is back a - gain.

Verse 2

Dark - ness is end - ded, ___ gone ___ the sad days.

Come light the lamps and let them spread their rays. ___

Ra - ma is ___ the king. ___

Peo - ple ___ of A - yo - dya ___ greet him.

Return to Chorus

Flow - ers we bring, let's dance ___ and ___ sing.

Divali

Fetch the candles.
Make it bright.
This is our festival
of light.

Lakshmi is coming
with luck and treats.
There's going to be laughter,
fireworks and sweets.

Family and friends
are together tonight.
For this is Divali,
our festival of light.

Tony Mitton

Dakshina and the Queen's necklace

Long ago in Rajasthan there lived a king named Kamal Singh. His kingdom was small but it was rich and prosperous. Even so, Kamal Singh was not satisfied. He was a very ambitious person and built up a large army. Kamal Singh was a powerful man, but he was also proud and foolish.

One day some spice merchants came from Kashmir with a large and valuable load of saffron. They wanted to sell the saffron to Kamal Singh and so, to show the merchants how rich he was, Kamal Singh bought it all and then ordered every sack to be thrown into a ditch.

His foolish action angered the goddess Lakshmi and she decided to teach the arrogant king a lesson. She made him a gambler. Soon Kamal Singh had lost all his money, but worse still he gambled his kingdom and lost that too. So, taking his son Ashvini and his daughter-in-law, Dakshina, with him he left his kingdom in humiliation and despair.

The three walked for many days till, footsore and weary, they came to the capital of another kingdom. Here they decided to stay for a while and try their luck. They built a tiny cottage on the edge of the city and Kamal Singh and Ashvini scraped together a living doing whatever work they could: carrying loads, drawing water or breaking stones.

Dakshina was a sensible, good-hearted girl. She worked hard, looked after their tiny home and was always bright and cheerful. She told her husband and Kamal Singh that as well as the little money they brought home each day they should bring something else too. The two agreed to her suggestion and each day brought something. It might be a log of wood, a lump of stone of brick or perhaps a few vegetables – anything they could lay hands on in fact.

But one day the only thing they could find was a dead snake. So, holding it by the tail, Ashvini carried it home where he threw it up on the cottage roof.

Next evening when father and son were on their way home there seemed to be much ado in the city. Kamal Singh asked what was going on.

'Haven't you heard?' a passer-by said. 'The Queen has lost her most precious necklace. She left it on the windowsill this morning and a kite swooped down, seized it in his claw and flew off. Now the king has announced that anyone who can recover the necklace will be richly rewarded.'

When Ashvini and Kamal Singh got home they told Dakshina what they'd heard. 'The Queen's necklace!' she cried in surprise. 'I think I have it.'

'You? How can you have it?' said her husband.

'How did you get it?' demanded Kamal Singh.

'I'm telling you, I do have the Queen's necklace,' replied Dakshina. 'Now quickly, go to the palace and find out what the reward is.'

Ashvini ran to the palace. 'What reward will be given to the finder of the Queen's necklace?' he called to the guards.

'Wait here. We will ask His Majesty,' they replied. Soon the guards returned.

'The King says he will give anything that you ask for, within reason,' they told Ashvini.

Ashvini went back to Dakshina and told her what the guards had said.

'Come on then. Hurry!' she replied. 'Let's go to the King.' So they hurried to the palace and asked to see the King.

'Is this Your Majesty's necklace?' Dakshina asked, holding the necklace out to the Queen.

'Yes, that's it!' cried the Queen in delight, 'but where did you find it?'

'It was like this,' went on Dakshina. 'This morning I was standing outside our cottage when a kite flew down on to the roof. In his beak was this necklace. Now on the roof was a dead snake. The bird dropped the necklace and, picking up the snake, flew off again.'

'What luck!' said the Queen. 'I thought I'd never see my favourite necklace again. Tell us, Dakshina, how can we reward you?'

'Well, Your Majesties,' replied Dakshina. 'If you please... it's not money I want, nor land. All I ask is this: on the night of Diwali, no house in the city, not even your royal palace, shall be lit with lamps. Moreover, all those who wish to light lamps should come to our cottage and light their lamps around it.'

This seemed a strange request to the King and Queen. They were unhappy about not lighting Diwali lamps but agreed to do as Dakshina asked. So, a royal announcement was made: 'On Diwali night all lamps are to be put up around Dakshina's cottage'.

After a few days it was the festival of Diwali. The only lamps in the city that evening were around Dakshina's cottage. When the goddess Lakshmi arrived to bless the houses with wealth and prosperity she could not see a single light. There seemed to be total darkness; no welcoming glimmer anywhere. She could not enter a single house. She searched to the north, south, east and west, then at last right on the very farthest edge of the city she saw a lighted cottage. Thinking that there at least she could spend the night, Lakshmi hurried towards it. But in the doorway she saw Dakshina standing holding a large stick.

'Stop!' cried Dakshina as Lakshmi tried to enter. 'You'll not shelter under THIS roof!'

'Whatever do you mean?' asked Lakshmi. 'Now tell me, young woman, why are all the other homes in this city in darkness. And how is it that when I come to bless you, you will not even allow me to enter your house?'

'Why should I let YOU in here?' demanded Dakshina. 'What have you done for us except make our lives a misery, and just because you lost your temper.'

'I promise to help you,' replied the goddess. 'Please let me spend the night in your cottage. I'll even get your kingdom back for you.'

'Very well,' smiled Dakshina and putting aside her stick she led Lakshmi into the cottage. There the goddess spent the night and she blessed Kamal Singh's humble home.

In the morning when Dakshina awoke, Lakshmi had gone but the cottage was filled with gold and precious stones. Not long after, Dakshina, Ashvini and Kamal Singh returned to their own kingdom and by and by they were able to recover all they had lost.

Renuka Singh

Diwali

Aayee Diwali aayee Diwali
Khūshiya(n) bhuri aayee Diwali
Southall noo jaawa(n)gay
Luddoo pay ray khaawa(n)gay
Gūrdwaray jaawa(n)gay
Mombutia(n) jugawa(n)gay
Putakay ghur liawa(n)gay
Tha tha kur chulawa(n)gay

Traditional Punjabi

Key
a = <u>a</u>t	ee = f<u>ee</u>t	oa = c<u>oa</u>t	ū = p<u>u</u>t
aa = c<u>a</u>r	i = p<u>i</u>n	oo = m<u>oo</u>n	u = b<u>u</u>t
ay = p<u>ay</u>	ia = famil<u>ia</u>r	ow = c<u>ow</u>	th = <u>th</u>in
e = b<u>e</u>t	o = g<u>o</u>t	oy = b<u>oy</u>	(n) = nasal sound

GURU PURB – GURU NANAK'S BIRTHDAY

Guru Purb or Guru Nanak's birthday is celebrated on the full moon day of November (although Nanak was actually born on 14th April) and is an important day for Sikhs. It commemorates the birthday of Guru Nanak, founder of the Sikh religion.

Guru Nanak Dev was born in 1469CE in the village of Talwadi (now in Pakistan and known as Nankana Sahib). His family were high caste Hindus. After a revelation at Sultanpur Nanak tried to unite Hindus and Muslims and made four journeys to spread the message he received from God.

The festival starts two days before full moon with a continuous reading of the Guru Granth Sahib in gurdwaras all over the world. The reading is done by a team of readers and finishes on the morning of the full moon day after which there is an act of worship. For the rest of the day stories about Guru Nanak, his teachings and experiences are told. Throughout the day a special 'Guru Purb' langar (free kitchen) is in operation at gurdwaras supplying food to the community.

Guru Purb – 1

Who was born
in Talwadi, in Talwadi?
Guru Nanak Dev!

Who grew tall
in Talwadi, in Talwadi?
Guru Nanak Dev!

Who travelled far
from Talwadi, from Talwadi?
Guru Nanak Dev!

Whose birth and life
do we remember?
Guru Nanak Dev!

Now we remember
Talwadi, Talwadi
and Guru Nanak Dev!

Judith Nicholls

Guru Purb – 2

Come to the gurdwara,
gather round;
gather, listen, worship
on the morning of full moon!

Come to the gurdwara,
gather round;
gather, celebrate the day
Guru Nanak was born!

Judith Nicholls

Nanak reborn

One day when Nanak went to bathe in the river he vanished. The servant who was with him looked but could see no sign of him; others searched and searched, his clothes were found but Nanak himself seemed to have completely disappeared. So everyone thought he had drowned. There was great mourning in Sultanpur.

Nanak was missing for three days and three nights but on the fourth day he returned home. People asked him where he had been but all he said was this: 'There is no Hindu; there is no Muslim.' At first everyone was puzzled but Nanak said that he had received a message from the one God and went on to explain that both Hindus and Muslims believe in God; both worship him and pray to him and both say that people should be good, kind and truthful. The only difference was that they said these things in different ways and this resulted in misery and unhappiness. Nanak wanted all people to be happy, to act like brothers, to love and respect one another and to serve God to the best of their ability.

Then Nanak told the chief of Sultanpur that he could no longer work for him, he now must serve only God. He gave away all his belongings and taking his servant, Mardana, with him set off to take God's truth to the people everywhere.

Colin J. Bennett

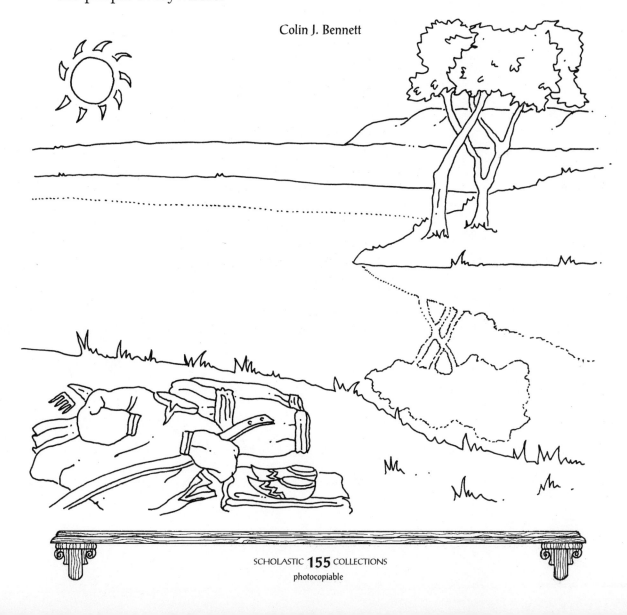

Guru Nanak

Nanak was a holy man
His birthday the Sikhs celebrate
They remember the light he brought to the world
Through what he taught and did.

He wanted all men to be brothers
To love one another and care,
So he journeyed both east and westward
With this message from God to share.

Now on a dark day in November
The Golden Temple is lit
With hundreds of lights and candles
While the Granth Sahib is read.

Class 4B

Guru Nanak's birthday

I'm blowing my pipe
for Guru Nanak –
blowing my pipe
today!

The band is out,
and the boys are wearing
all their best
array.

The priests are reading
the holy book,
and soon, when they reach
the end,

We'll be feasting, all,
at the Festival!
Sit down and eat,
my friend!

Jean Kenward

The wealthy banker of Lahore

Once, long ago, there lived a banker in the city of Lahore. His name was Duni Chand, and he was well known throughout the city for his greed and dishonesty. He lived in a beautiful palace, which shone with gold, marble and precious jewels.

One day, Duni Chand learnt that Guru Nanak had arrived in the city. At once Duni Chand rushed to find the Guru, so that he could invite him to a special feast in the Guru's honour. Guru Nanak accepted the invitation and preparations for the feast began.

It was a splendid occasion. Tasty dishes were set before the guests and in the background minstrels played soft music. The guests all agreed that it was a magnificent feast. When everyone had finished, Duni Chand turned to Guru Nanak. 'I am a wealthy man,' he said. 'If I can do anything for you, please tell me.'

Guru Nanak sat for a moment, deep in thought. He looked around at the splendour of the palace, the rich tapestries hanging on the wall and the fine golden dishes. Then, fumbling in his pocket, he drew out a slim case which contained a tiny, fine needle.

'Yes, there is something I would like you to do for me,' he replied, holding up the needle. 'I would like you to keep this needle very safely and give it back when we meet in the next world.' And with these words, the Guru left the feast.

Duni Chand felt full of importance. The Guru had entrusted him with such a special task. He took the needle and showed it to his wife, explaining what the Guru had told him. To his utter astonishment, she burst into peals of laughter.

'Oh my poor husband,' she laughed. 'I should go back and ask Guru Nanak how you can take it to heaven with you.'

Feeling rather confused, Duni Chand hurried after the Guru, who was just disappearing around the corner of the street. 'Guru Nanak, Guru Nanak,' he called. 'Please tell me one thing before you go. How can I take this needle with me when I die?'

The Guru looked at Duni Chand kindly and said, 'If you cannot take a tiny needle with you when you die, how are you going to take all your riches? You will only be remembered for the good things you have done in this world when you go to the next.'

Duni Chand thought and realised the truth in the Guru's words. He felt ashamed of his actions and from that day on, he and his wife used their wealth to help the poor.

Rani and Jugnu Singh

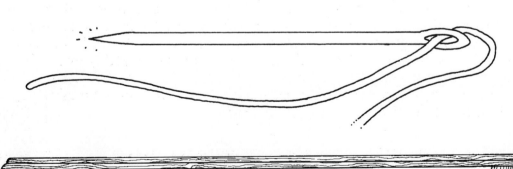

HANUKKAH

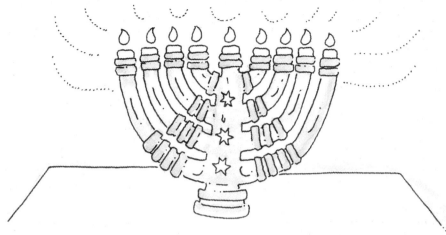

Hanukkah (also spelt Chanukah or Hannukah) is the Jewish festival of light. It is an eight-day festival which begins on the 25th of the month of Kislev (November or December). It celebrates the victory of Judah Maccabee over Antiochus, a Syrian king. The Syrians had abused the Jewish temple, putting statues there, sacrificing pigs and forbidding the Jews to worship there, but the Jews were determined to regain their temple and under Maccabee they succeeded. They found just enough oil to keep the temple lamp going for one day so the menorah was lit even though it was only expected to burn for the day. However, the oil lasted for not one but eight days, enough time for new oil to be made.

Now the festival of Hanukkah candles, which means dedication, celebrates this wonder. The central focus of each of the eight days of the festival is the lighting of the Hanukkah. In Jewish homes and synagogues an eight-branched candle stick or menorah is lit – one candle being lit each evening until on the eighth day all the candles are burning. (Sometimes there is a ninth candle holder to hold the 'servant' candle used to light the others.) Special prayers are said and songs sung. Synagogues hold parties on the Sabbath and a special game of spinning the dreidel is played. This is also sometimes given to children. The dreidel, a small spinning top, has four sides, each marked with one of the Hebrew letters N G H or Sh (*nun gimmel hay shin*). The meaning of the letters are in the saying '*Nes gadol haya sham*' – a great miracle happened there.

Food cooked in oil, such as potato latkes (a kind of pancake), is traditionally eaten as a reminder of the miracle of the oil in the temple. Cheese is another of the special foods eaten at Hanukkah; this custom comes from the story of a very brave Jewish woman called Judith who saved an entire town by serving a Syrian general with a meal rich in cheeses. This made him very thirsty and to quench his thirst Judith gave him wine, so much that he fell into a drunken sleep and Judith killed him, causing his army to flee for their lives.

Greetings cards are sent and presents are often given, sometimes one for each night of the festival.

Hanukka candles

David Moses

2. Songs to be sung and prayers to be prayed.
Presents to be given and games to be played.
Spinning the dreidel, where will it stop?
Half, all or nothing on the spinning of a top.

3. Blessings recited, tales to be read of
Battles that were fought and blood that was shed
Saving the Temple, making it fit for the
Oil in the lamp of the Lord to be lit.

4. Wine to be tasted, food to be shared.
Fresh potato pancakes to be prepared.
Being together, family and friends
Hanukka gelt for children to spend.

5. Lit from the centre, added from the right,
Eight Hanukka candles burning bright.
Shamash, the servant, that makes nine
Blazing their message 'til the end of time.

Chorus
Hanukka, a great thanksgiving and
Hanukka, a brand new start
Filling us with the joy of living and the
Light that shines from a loving heart.

Hanukkah O Hanukkah

Esther L. Nelson

O Han - uk - kah, O Han - uk - kah, a yon - tef a

shey - ner, A lus - tig - er, a frey - lich - er, ni - to noch a -

zein - er. Al - e nacht in dreyd - lach shpi - len __ mir

Zu - dig hey - se lat - kes est on a shir. Gesh - vin - der, tzindt

kin - der, di din - in - ke lich - tel - ech on. Zul

ye - der ba - zund - er ba - zing - en dem vun - der Un

kumt al - le tant - sen in kon. _____ Zul

ye - der ba - zund - er ba - zing - en dem vun - der Un

kumt al - le tant - sen in kon. _____

If you want to sing it in English, you can sing:

O Hanukkah, O Hanukkah, a festival of joy,
A holiday, a jolly day, for every girl and boy.
Spin the whirling dreidel all week long.
Eat the sizzling latkes, sing the happy songs!
Now light then, tonight then, the flickering candles in a row,
Retell the wondrous story of God in all His glory,
And dance by the candles' cheering glow.

Hannuka

God's Spirit in the temple will stay,
As the sacred lamp shines every day,
But the King of Syria let its brightness fade,
When to worship their God, the Jews were forbade.

So the angry Jews cried, 'This King we'll fight,
And we shall be victorious and the lamp we'll light,'
But after the fight, they had oil for one day,
So with faith they lit it without delay.

For eight days it shone; the Lord was near,
When fresh oil was brought, how the people did cheer,
The temple was cleaned and all went so well,
This wonderful story our children we tell.

When Hannuka comes it's a time of great joy,
For no one our faith dares to destroy,
Each evening our mother a candle will light,
Until eight flames quiver for our delight.

Janet E. Greenyer

Joshua's gelt

It was a very cold December morning as Joshua walked to school. He was looking forward to the weekend with great anticipation. In two evenings it would be the first night of Chanukah. Chanukah was always special since it brought so much happiness at this time of year. Also, on the night of the first candle, he usually received a very nice present. Then, every night for the rest of the holiday, his parents would give him 'Chanukah gelt' after lighting the candles. Even his aunts, uncles and grandparents had 'gelt' (coins) for him.

This morning, Joshua was engrossed in thoughts of his new Chanukah presents when a classmate ran past him. As Jeremy whizzed by, he flipped Joshua's scarf forward.

'Hey Josh, race you to class,' he yelled. Joshua had just enough time to break into a fast run and he caught up to Jeremy when they reached the door.

'Darn, even with a head-start, I can't out-race you,' pouted Jeremy.

'Well,' answered Joshua, 'keep trying. There is always a chance.'

'Yeah, and I know one way I can always beat you. I always get better presents. After all, your holiday is only a copy of my holiday. So mine is better. Ha! Ha! Ha!' sneered Jeremy, as he ran off before Joshua could answer. All day Joshua carried around a feeling about the remark that Jeremy had made. Of course, he was only being mean, Joshua tried to tell himself. But, why do I feel so bad now, when I felt so good before?

After school, he slowly walked to Hebrew classes, feeling the sun on his face. It was still cold out, but the sun warmed him a bit. Inside there was a chill that he could not understand. He always loved Chanukah, so why was he so upset when Jeremy said presents weren't really part of Chanukah, and that it was a copy of his holiday? He had always received gifts and Chanukah gelt too.

In Rabbi Goldman's class, Joshua could not concentrate on the lesson, and was startled to hear his name called out.

'Joshua, please wake up and pay attention to class,' reprimanded the Rabbi. 'If you have a problem, please speak up!'

His thoughts bothered him so much that he decided to tell the Rabbi and share them with the class. '...And when he said it wasn't really for Chanukah, I was upset,' finished Joshua.

'I'm glad you brought this up, Joshua,' answered Rabbi Goldman. 'Giving presents on Chanukah is really a relatively modern custom, but giving Chanukah gelt is as old as Chanukah itself. The coins were very important to the Maccabees. After winning their freedom for Syrian rule, they created their own government and monetary system. The Jewish people in Modiin minted their own coins – money. Many of these coins had menorahs and other Chanukah symbols printed on them: symbols of freedom, of the miracle of light, and of the right to pray as Jews. These are all part of the celebration of Chanukah.'

'Over the years, especially in Europe, Russia, Poland and Spain, parents gave their children coins for Chanukah. So, we have Chanukah Gelt – or money – that is as old as the miracle of light,' explained Rabbi Goldman. 'Does that help answer your questions?' he asked.

'Yes,' responded Joshua, 'but what about presents? They are new. What does that mean?"

The Rabbi smiled, as he continued his answer to Joshua's weighty problem. 'You see, Joshua, things change over the years. Customs are different all over the world. Just like there are a vast variety of menorah designs, so there are many special foods and customs celebrated by Jews all over the world. Each family does it a little differently, but all celebrate the Chanukah festival with lights, gifts or coins, food and dreydel games.

Today parents give gifts because they have become easier to buy, or make, than in olden times. Now gifts have become a custom added to all the beautiful things that we do to celebrate Chanukah.'

'So, it really is a Chanukah custom to get gifts,' repeated Joshua excitedly.

'Yes,' said the Rabbi. 'Chanukah presents for children and even adults are part of the celebration of Chanukah. They have become as important as Chanukah gelt, latkes, dreydel games and the eight nights of lighting candles.'

The excitement of the morning was back with Joshua. He felt happy again. In less than two days he would get to sing the blessing over the candles and share the joy that would last for eight nights with each added candle. This year he would have extra fun, because he knew the reason for all the customs.

'Good night, Rabbi Goldman,' yelled Joshua as he ran out of the front door of the building, 'and thank you for a happy Chanukah!'

Jacqueline Jacobson Pliskin

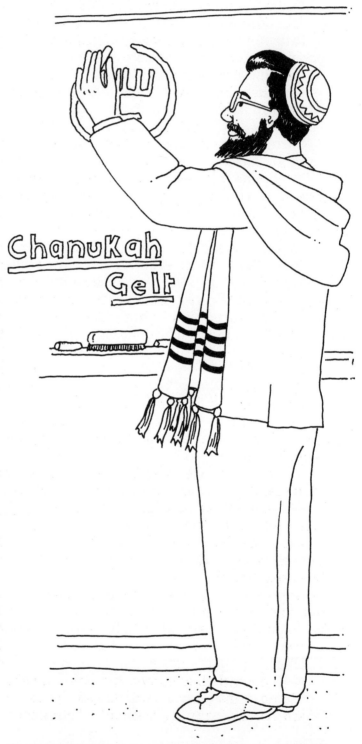

Just enough is plenty

Malka's family lived in a village in Poland. They were poor, but not so poor. They had candles for the Sabbath, noisemakers for Purim, and spinning tops for Chanukah.

Mama was busy preparing for tonight, the first of the eight nights of Chanukah. She peeled onions and grated potatoes for the latkes, the potato pancakes.

Malka's younger brother Zalman carved a dreidel, a spinning top.

'This dreidel will spin the fastest of all,' he boasted.

Papa was working long hours in his tailor shop so they could buy more food for the holiday. More potatoes, more onions, more flour, more oil.

For on the first night of Chanukah, Malka's family always invited many guests. But this year only Aunt Hindy and Uncle Shmuel were coming to visit.

'Only two guests?' Malka asked. 'Last year, we had so many guests that Papa had to put boards over the pickle barrels to make the table big enough.'

'That was last year,' Mama said gently. 'This year has not been a good one for Papa in the shop. People bring him just a little mending here, a little mending there. He cannot afford to buy new material to sew fancy holiday dresses and fine suits.'

'But it's Chanukah,' Malka reminded Mama.

Mama patted Malka's shoulder. 'Don't worry, Malkaleh. We know how to stretch. We're poor, but not so poor. Now go. Ask Papa if he has a few more coins. I need more eggs for the latkes.'

Malka bundled up in her jacket and shawl, her scarf and boots. It was cold and snowy and so windy. The wind chased her all the way to the marketplace.

She raced into Papa's shop. 'Mama sent me to buy more eggs.'

'More eggs. More this, more that. Soon there will be no kopeks left. Not even one for Chanukah money.'

Malka stood still in the doorway. No Chanukah money! Was Papa joking? How could she and Zalman play the dreidel game without even a kopek?

'Malka, don't just stand there. Here. Go buy the eggs,' Papa said. 'And quickly. Aunt Hindy and Uncle Shmuel will be here soon.'

The coins that Papa gave her for the eggs jingled inside her pocket as she ran. Clink. Clink.

Last year, Malka used her Chanukah money to buy candy treats at the marketplace and sleigh rides around the village. Clink. Clink. But this was egg money.

Malka carried the eggs carefully back to the house. She burst into tears when she saw Mama.

'Papa doesn't even have a kopek left for us,' she wailed. 'No Chanukah money.'

'Did Papa say that?'

Malka nodded. Her chin quivered and she couldn't say another word.

Mama wiped her hands on her apron and hugged Malka close. 'Was there ever a Chanukah without a kopek for a child to play dreidel with?'

Malka shrugged. She didn't know.

Suddenly, there were loud noises at the door: horses whinnying and stomping and people shouting, 'Happy Chanukah!'

'It's them!' Mama cried. 'And the latkes aren't fried yet.' She ran to the door to welcome Aunt Hindy and Uncle Shmuel, and then she hurried back into the kitchen to fry latkes.

When she finished, she put a coin in the charity box on the shelf, just as she did before each holiday and Sabbath. Malka saw her.

'What if that's our last kopek?' Malka whispered to Zalman.

Then Papa came in from the shop, and the whole family gathered around the little brass menorah on the windowsill.

Papa picked up the shammash, the special candle at the top of the menorah, and chanted the familiar prayers. 'Blessed is God who commanded us to light the Chanukah candle.... Blessed is God who worked miracles for our ancestors long ago....'

Zalman tugged at Malka's sleeve. 'What miracles?' he asked in a whisper.

'You remember. The oil in the Temple. The oil that burned for eight days instead of only one,' Malka explained quickly.

When Papa finished the blessing, he used the shammash to light the first candle-holder in the menorah. The other seven candle-holders were empty, waiting for their turn on the nights to come.

'Sit down, everyone.' Mama said, and rushed into the kitchen.

Malka carried platters of latkes to the table as soon as Mama filled them. She saw Papa give Zalman the warning eye as Zalman piled six latkes on his plate.

Papa came into the kitchen. 'Is there enough?' he whispered to Mama.

'Just enough,' said Mama.

When Malka put the last latke on the table, she and Papa and Mama sat down, too. There was a knock on the door. 'Did you invite anyone else?' asked Mama.

'No,' said Papa. He got up to see who was there.

It was a pedlar with a large sack on his back. He had white hair and wore a wrinkled black greatcoat and torn boots.

'I saw the Chanukah lights in your window.' He spoke softly with his head bowed.

Mama stood up and went to the door. 'Come in. Join us. Just like Abraham and Sarah in the Bible, we always have something for the stranger who knocks on our door.'

Papa gave Mama a worried look. So did Malka. 'We can stretch the "just enough",' Mama whispered to them. 'We're poor, but not so poor.'

Mama gave the old man one of her latkes. So did Papa. So did Malka, Aunt Hindy, Uncle Shmuel and even Zalman.

Everyone ate the latkes with apple sauce and sour cream.

'I'm finished, Papa,' said Zalman. 'Can I play dreidel?'

'Dreidel. I haven't played dreidel in years.' The old man leaned forward and beckoned Zalman closer with his finger. 'Do you have one?'

'The fastest one in my class,' Zalman said.

The old man looked at Papa. 'I have a few kopeks. The children could use them to play the dreidel game.'

Malka was glad and thanked the pedlar. Now she would have a kopek to play with. But still no candy treats or sleigh rides. No cousins or friends to fill the house.

Malka and Zalman sat on the floor. So did the old man. He took turns with the dreidel, too.

Spin.

Shin. Put one in the pile.

Twirl.

Hay. Take half the coins.

Spin again.

Nun. Take nothing.

Twirl again.

Gimmel. Take all.

Just like the children, the old man made a face when the top landed on *nun*, nothing, and he laughed when the top stopped on *gimmel*, take all.

Then he taught the children songs with words that went around and around again. Once he sang the words loudly and happily, and once he hummed the tune quietly with his eyes closed.

Oy chiri biri biri bim bum bum,
Oy chiri biri biri bim bum bum.

Still singing, he grabbed their hands and they danced in circles, whirling like dreidels themselves.

Giggling and huffing, Malka and Zalman fell to the floor.

The old man reached into his pedlar's sack and drew out one book and then another. He read the stories in his soft voice. Some of them made Malka laugh, others brought tears to her eyes. His stories were about kind people and cruel people, about angels and wonder-working rabbis, about beggars and miracles.

Of all the stories, her favourites were the ones about Elijah the Prophet, who would come back to earth to help someone who was poor but kind-hearted. One time Elijah dressed as a horseman, one time as a beggar, one time as a magician.

'It's as if the whole house were filled with guests,' Malka told the pedlar. 'With the people of your stories.'

Later that night, after Aunt Hindy and Uncle Shmuel left, Papa made a sleeping place for the pedlar. He piled straw by the stove. Before they went to sleep, the old man gave each child a kopek to keep.

'For your Chanukah money,' he said. 'For some candy treats and sleigh rides around the village.'

Malka laughed. 'How did you know?'

The pedlar smiled. 'I know.'

Then Malka and Zalman tumbled into their beds along one of the kitchen walls.

'Good night, Reb... Oh, I don't even know your name,' Malka said.

'I'll tell you tomorrow,' the old man answered.

When Malka awoke in the morning, she lay still in her bed, remembering her dreams about cruel kings and kind farmers, about the people in the pedlar's stories.

'I especially liked the stories about Elijah,' Malka said softly, hoping the old man was awake, too. But when she looked for him, she saw an empty pile of straw. He was gone.

'Mama! Papa! Zalman!' Malka called. 'Come quickly. The pedlar is gone.'

She thought of the winter wind pushing him down the street.

'Oh, I wished he had stayed. Didn't he know Mama can always make plenty out of just enough?' she said to Zalman, who looked disappointed too. 'And we don't even know his name.'

'But wait,' Mama said. 'What's that over there? Did he forget something?'

Malka saw the pedlar's sack by the door and ran over to it.

'There's a note,' she said. 'Mama, what does it say?'

'Just "Happy Chanukah. This will help you,"' Mama read.

'No name?'

'No. No name.'

Malka peeped into the sack. She recognised the book on top. It was the old book with the stories about Elijah.

Malka gasped. Clutching the book, she turned to Mama and Papa and Zalman, 'I know who the pedlar is. He's Elijah!'

'Elijah? You really believe that old man is Elijah the Prophet? Oy,' Papa said, hitting his head with his hand.

'He could be, Papa,' Malka said. 'Remember how Elijah left things for the people he visited in those stories?'

'But we are real people, not story-people, Malkaleh. And why would he leave us his whole sackful of books? I'm a tailor, not a book pedlar.'

Papa turned to the sack. He took out one book after the other, big books and little books, old books and new books. About halfway down the sack, Papa stopped. He stood up, confused.

'There's a problem?' Mama asked anxiously.

'No, not a problem,' Papa said hesitantly. 'Just...'

Once again he stooped down over the sack. They all crowded around him as he lifted one, two, three bolts of silk and more out of the sack. Purple silk, green silk, dotted silk, silk with stripes and checks and flowers.

'Look what your Elijah gave us this Chanukah!' Papa said to Malka and twirled her happily in the air. 'What fancy holiday dresses and fine suits I can make now.'

He took Malka's hand and Malka took Zalman's hand and Zalman reached over for Mama. Malka turned to Mama and said, 'I'm glad you're so good at making just enough be plenty!'

Laughing, they all began to dance, and sing,

Oy chiri biri biri bim bum bum,
Oy chiri biri biri bim bum bum,
Oy chiri biri biri bim.

Barbara Diamond Goldin

Hanukah

Hanukah, Hanukah,
Festival of light.
Candles burn, tops spin round,
Time of great delight.
Hanukah, Hanukah,
Let us dance and sing.
Candles burn, guests come in,
Presents they will bring.

Traditional Jewish song

My Hanukkah candles

Eight little candles
All in a line;
Eight little candles
Glitter and shine.

Eight little candles,
Each little flame
Whispers a legend
Of honour and fame.

Eight little candles,
Sparklets of gold,
Stories of battles
And heroes of old.

'Courage, but courage,
Maccabee's brave son,
Fight for light –
And the battle is won.'

Philip M. Raskin

Hanukkah for hope

One candle
now begins a glimmering flame
Two candles
children play the dreidle game
Three candles
we can laugh, enjoy our sweets
Four candles
give thanks for good things to eat
Five candles
mother makes latkes, fries them in oil
Six candles
we remember God's mercy awhile
Seven candles
now Hanukkah is almost past
Eight candles
remind us miracles can last

Our Menorah shines complete,
God's goodness
Hope at Hanukkah.

Chris Riley

Dreidel song

Twirl about, dance about,
Spin, spin, spin!
Turn, Dreidel, turn –
Time to begin!

Soon it is Hanukkah –
Fast, Dreidel, fast!
For you will lie still
When Hanukkah's past.

Efraim Rosenzweig

CHRISTMAS

Christmas or Christ's Mass is the Christian festival when the birth of Jesus, whom Christians believe to be the Son of God, is celebrated. Where the Gregorian calendar is used Christmas Day always falls on December 25th. Although it is not known when the birth of Jesus actually did take place it is thought to have been during a winter season in the reign of the Roman emperor, Augustus. Thus by commemorating Jesus' birth in mid-winter Christians were celebrating at about the same time as ancient pagans held their feast for the winter solstice (21st December) and many of the customs associated with Christmas are of pagan origin.

Nowadays Christmas is celebrated in different ways by Christian communities all over the world but the fundamental belief of all Christians about Christmas is that of Incarnation. Stories are told of the Virgin Mary giving birth to Jesus in a stable, and of the shepherds and the three wise men or kings who came to worship and honour him. The festival of Epiphany, twelve days after Christmas (January 6th) is the day Christians remember the arrival of the kings at the stable. Their gifts, described in the Gospel of St. Matthew, were symbolic: gold showed Jesus was a king; frankincense is associated with worship; myrrh, spice often used in the burial of the dead, showed that Jesus was to suffer.

Christmas is also celebrated as a festival of light. Candles are used to symbolise the light of truth in Christ and his teachings and to show the Christian view of Jesus as 'the light of the world'. In some parts of India, Christians use divas at Advent to symbolise lighting the way for the coming of Christ at Christmas.

Mrs O'Deary

Debbie Campbell

Gently

Intro:

1. There's an old wo-man who lives in our street, She does-n't have mon-ey for nice things to eat, So give her a pres-ent or give her a call, Or she won't have a Christ-mas at all. _____ So give her a pres-ent or give her a

call   Or she won't have a   Christ-mas at   all.

2. Mrs O'Deary is ninety years old.
She cannot walk far and she suffers from cold.
I hope Father Christmas will give her a call,
Or she won't have a Christmas at all.
I hope Father Christmas will give her a call,
Or she won't have a Christmas at all.

A village Christmas

A story from North India

'How's that!' shouted Sumit. 'Out!' cried the rest of the boys, and their friend Ram gave up his bat to the next one in.

The bat was a piece of wood, cut to shape; the ball was rubber, and the wickets were a few bricks. The boys all went to the village school, and Sumit and Ram were special friends. The last term in the school year had finished the day before and the boys had a whole week's holiday to celebrate the Christian festival of Christmas, and the New Year. Every day they played cricket on the hard-baked mud of the village street, running barefoot; they only stopped their game for meal-time at midday.

Sumit and Ram lived in mud-built houses with slate roofs. Their fathers worked on the land growing rice, and during the busy seasons the two boys also went to the fields to help. A bad harvest meant less food, less clothes and less money for the family, so everybody joined in to help when necessary. This year the harvest, which had just been gathered, had been a good one and the two families had much to celebrate. There was one difference between them, however: Sumit's family was Christian and Ram's Hindu.

The next day would be Christmas Day and Ram was very anxious to know what Sumit and his family would be doing then.

'Will you be out to play cricket tomorrow?' he asked.

'Oh, no!' replied Sumit. 'It's Christmas Day. Tell you what, why don't you come to our house tonight and stay over until tomorrow. Then you could see what we do at Christmas. It would be super if you could.'

'I'd love that,' said Ram. 'Wait a minute, I'll go and ask my father.' So Ram rushed home, bursting with excitement. 'Father, can I go to Sumit's house tonight and stay till tomorrow, to see how they celebrate Christmas?'

'Of course you can, son,' replied his father. 'I should like to hear all about it when you come back. After all, Sumit came here when we had our festival, didn't he?'

Later that afternoon Ram went to Sumit's house, taking with him some sweetmeats for Sumit's mother. He found Sumit and his little sister Sushila dancing up and down with excitement. The house was full of a delicious smell of cooking, and their father had just come home from the market, carrying some parcels. He gave one each to Sumit and Sushila, and another to their mother.

Ram watched as they opened their parcels. In Sumit's there was a new blue shirt; Sushila's contained a bright yellow dress; and in their mother's there was a red sari. They were all delighted with their presents.

'Do you always have new clothes for Christmas, like we do for our festivals?' Ram asked Sumit.

'Yes, if we are lucky,' replied Sumit. 'Last year we couldn't because we had a bad harvest and there wasn't enough money.'

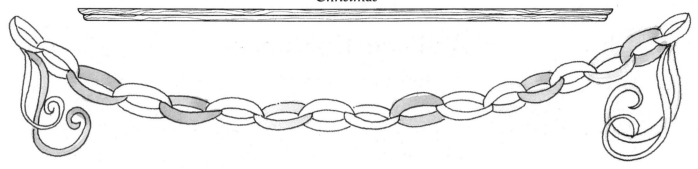

They both noticed that there were two more parcels which hadn't been opened. 'What's in those, Father?' asked Sumit.

'Look!' said Father, and from one bag he took rolls of coloured paper and from the other two long, white candles.

'Oh!' cried Sumit and Sushila, clapping their hands. 'We can decorate the house.'

'What are the candles for?' asked Ram.

'Wait and see!' said Basanta Babu, which was what everyone called Sumit's father.

The three children sat down on the floor of the veranda. With paste and the rolls of coloured paper they made long strings of paper chains – red, yellow, green and blue. Then, with Father's help, they hung the paper chains round the veranda and the room inside. It looked very gay.

Ram noticed that Basanta Babu had placed a small table against one of the walls. Above the table hung a cross, and on the table was a pretty, white lace cloth. There was an open book and a gaily coloured greeting card with a picture of a young husband and wife, a baby lying in a cow's feeding trough, and several animals looking at the baby. On each side of the book was a white candle, and at the front of the table there were incense sticks on a stand.

'What is the book and what is the picture about?' asked Ram.

'The book is the Bible, which contains our Holy Scriptures, and the picture is of the birth of Jesus Christ. Tomorrow we celebrate his birthday,' answered Basanta Babu.

Ram was pleased to know what Christmas was about, and he listened carefully to all that Sumit's father told him, so that he could tell them at home.

By this time it was getting dark and Sumit's mother lit the hurricane lanterns. She placed one on the steps leading on to the veranda and the other inside the house.

Basanta Babu was one of the best-known Christians in the district. He was very popular, and was secretary of the local church.

Sumit began to get excited, and soon Ram realised why. Men - young and older – began to arrive at the house. Several of them were carrying musical instruments – a violin, drums, rattles, and small cymbals.

'What are they going to do?' whispered Ram to Sumit.

'They are going out to sing Christmas songs around the village,' replied Sumit.

More and more people arrived until the little house was full. When everyone was there, Basanta Babu lit the incense sticks and then the candles, which made the room glow with light. He read the story of Christmas from the Bible, and then prayed, asking God's blessing on their carol singing and on their celebration of Christmas. When the prayer was finished, Sumit's mother came in, carrying plates of curry puffs and sweetmeats and cups of steaming tea.

It was past the children's bedtime, but no one thought of bed on Christmas Eve! Soon the men stood up and prepared for their journey which would take them around their own village and on to another one not far away. Laughing and talking they set out and soon their singing could be heard, accompanied by the drums and cymbals and other musical instruments. The songs told the story of the birth of Christ.

The singing continued for most of the night as the carol singers went from house to house. The sound gradually got fainter and fainter as the group moved farther off and finally went into the next village. At last Ram, Sumit and Sushila, exhausted by all the excitement, fell asleep on the mat on the floor. But at sunrise they were up again.

'Happy Christmas, children!' said Mother.

'Happy Christmas, Mother!' they replied.

'Hurry up, now. Put on your new clothes. We must get to church early to find a space,' she said.

They were soon ready, looking very smart. Ram put on a clean shirt and went with them. On the way to church they met many of their friends, all going the same way, and calling out, 'Happy Christmas!'. Ram felt excited and joined in with Sumit and his family as they replied, 'Happy Christmas!'

When they arrived, the church was already full. It was decorated with paper chains and stars and the words 'Happy Christmas!' were stuck on the wall. Suddenly everyone stood up and turned towards the door as the minister appeared, leading the group of men who had spent all night going around the villages. They were still singing and everyone joined in the hymn, praising God. The church was packed, and there were crowds outside, too.

Ram didn't understand much of the service, but he felt happy because everyone was smiling. After the service they went home. Friends and relatives came to wish Sumit's family a Happy Christmas, and his mother was kept busy offering Christmas cake, sweetmeats and tea to the visitors.

'Everyone seems so happy,' said Ram.

'Yes,' replied Sumit. 'Jesus Christ is born today. This is the good news which brings us such joy.'

It was well after midday before they all sat down to a delicious meal of rice and meat curry.

'I've had a wonderful time,' said Ram. 'When I go home this afternoon I shall have so much to tell my family.'

Just before sunset, Sumit's family set out to visit relations. But first they took Ram home, gave his parents some sweetmeats and wished them the joy of Christmas, for they believed that Jesus Christ was born for everyone.

Sumit – pronounced Shoemeet;
Ram – pronounced Raam;
Sushila – pronounced Shoesheila;
Basanta Babu – pronounced Boshonto Baaboo (o as in 'got').

Jean Stolton

from 'Christmas everywhere'

Everywhere, everywhere, Christmas tonight!
Christmas in lands of the fir-tree and pine,
Christmas in lands of the palm-tree and vine,
Christmas where snow-peaks stand solemn and white,
Christmas where cornfields lie sunny and bright,
Everywhere, everywhere, Christmas tonight!

Phillip Brooks

Christmas in two lands

There it is cold, or there is snow –
And holly, fires and mistletoe,
And carols sung out in the street
By children, walking through the sleet.
Church bells break the frozen air
Ringing loudly everywhere.
There is where white wonder glory
Comes to tell the Christmas story.

Here it is hot, the sun is gold –
And turns tired when the day is old.
Christmas carols are sung at night
Somewhere outside, by candle-light.
Church bells ring out in the heat
And call to people in the street.
The Christmas story here is told
In summer, when the sun is gold.

Joan Mellings

Rock a little baby

David Moses

Camel caravan song

Debbie Campbell

Mysteriously

Intro:

Late one night I saw three wise men, trav-el-lers — in the sand. Sil - hou - ette on the ho - ri - zon, ca - mel car - a - van. Straight a - head they rode that night, tur - ning nei - ther left nor right. Gui - ded by a shi - ning light, — ca - mel car - a - van. Trav-el-lers in — the sand,

The star

The long ribbon of road stretched out in front of them. It was dark and the concrete strip was picked up in the beam from the headlights of the car: it seemed to unroll for mile after mile without ending.

'I'm tired,' yawned Michael.

'I'm bored,' growled Gillian.

'And stiff,' went on Michael.

'For goodness' sake, shut up, you two. How do you think I feel, having to drive all this way?' said Father, twitching at the wheel so that the car took the slight bend in the motorway and avoided the green cats-eyes of the turning off.

'Perhaps we should have gone off the motorway at that junction,' said Mother. 'Everything is so black we seem to be getting absolutely nowhere.'

'We set off too late as usual,' snarled Father. 'A good job you telephoned to say they were not to worry if we didn't turn up until breakfast-time tomorrow.'

'Then let's agree,' said Mother, trying to smooth out ruffled tempers, 'that at the next junction we turn off and find somewhere to stay the night.'

It was Christmas Eve and the Johnson family were on their way up North to spend the holidays with grandparents. It had been, for them, a normal getaway. Father was late from the office; Michael and Gillian took ages to get ready; and Mother kept on finding things to do and to pack. The truth was, they all left things to the last minute and they were too late setting off for the two hundred mile drive. It was now nearly ten o'clock and still a hundred miles to go.

'Agreed,' they all said, and within a few minutes the blue and white sign was telling them that the next junction was one mile ahead. The mile went by and Father pulled the car to the left and up the slip road.

'Which way at the top?' he called.

'Left,' said Michael.

'Right,' said Gillian at the same time.

'Decide when we come to the top,' said Mother, and as Father slowed down they could see the names on the sign ahead picked out in the headlights: Low Row one way and Ayton Rudby the other.

'Let's try Ayton Rudby,' said Father, and he turned right, along a narrow country road. The black hedges seemed to close in on them as they drove along.

It was only a few minutes before they saw, lit up by the headlights, a sign which read: 'The Star Inn, one hundred yards ahead', followed almost immediately by the black silhouette of a building standing on a bend in the road.

'It's worth trying here,' said Father, and he pulled into an open space at the side of the building and slowed to a stop. Four pairs of eyes looked out at the darkened building.

'Is it open?' asked Mother anxiously.

'Surely they don't close so early on Christmas Eve!' said Father.

'Let's go and find out,' said Michael. He opened the car door letting in a cold blast of fresh air.

One by one they picked their way across the rather uneven ground to the front of the building. Not a soul was about but a yellow glow came from the windows: someone was inside.

By comparison with the darkness outside, the dim lighting inside seemed quite bright; the room looked warm and comfortable. The bar semi-circled one corner and the bottles and glasses winked back the red and yellow of a huge log fire that burned in the open hearth on one side of the room. There was no other lighting except for six or eight candles that burned in holders set on the round wooden tables in the middle of the room. It was all very warm and cosy and inviting, except that there was no one there: the place was deserted.

Father coughed and called out, 'Anybody there?' There was a shuffling and through a door that no one had noticed came a large, red-faced man. He had a kindly look about him but seemed surprised that someone had called out.

'Oh, hello,' he said. 'I thought I heard voices. You've come, then?'

'Well, yes,' said Father, 'but you can't have been expecting us....'

He was about to explain how they had just decided to turn off the motorway and had come

unexpectedly upon the inn when the man went out, 'Oh, aye; they said somebody would turn up sooner or later.'

Michael and Gillian looked at each other. Father and Mother looked at each other. There was something strange about it all, but what was it? Here was a country inn on Christmas Eve with no one except for a large red-faced man who seemed to be expecting them!

'We were wondering if you could put us up for the night,' said Mother. 'But I'm sure that's quite impossible.'

'Ah, well,' said the man. 'We are very busy, but it so happens that I have two rooms to spare, if the young lady and gentleman there don't mind sharing.'

They all looked round the empty room and wondered where the busyness might be, but no one made any comment until Father said, 'Right. Thank you. We'll take the two rooms.'

'Could you make us some tea or cocoa?' asked Mother, and the man said that he could. It was arranged that they should come back to the bar parlour for cocoa and biscuits after they had carried their cases upstairs and been shown their rooms.

It had been a long day and tiredness came suddenly upon them all. Within less than half an hour they were all in bed asleep.

What it was that awoke Michael he would never know. But whatever it was, he was awake, wide awake! As he sat up in bed he felt, rather than knew, that something was happening outside. Quietly he got out of bed and tiptoed to the window. The moon was up and the countryside was bathed in a grey-white light. He looked out and what he saw made him turn and whisper as loudly as he dared, 'Gillian, come and look. Gillian....'

Gillian woke at once and crept over to the window. 'What is it?' she asked.

'Well,' said Michael, 'I'm not sure, but it looks like a lot of people down in the courtyard, almost as if... as if... .'

'Almost as if we were watching a television play,' said Gillian quickly.

Kneeling at the low casement, they gazed out of the window and below them saw the crowd move away

leaving a young couple standing alone in the centre of the space. They made their way to the door. Soundlessly they knocked and the door was opened by the landlord who had served supper to the Johnsons earlier. The children saw him shake his head and then point to the back of the house. The young man gave a weary shrug of his shoulders and the couple turned away to an outbuilding which leaned against the long wall of the inn. The landlord shut the door and the couple disappeared inside the lean-to.

Everything seemed still. Michael and Gillian continued to watch. For how long they stared at the empty courtyard they did not know. Perhaps they dozed off. But then they saw other figures below. Men in a hurry, looking, knocking, and then finding what they were looking for and going, one by one, into the lean-to building. There were other figures, tall and stately, moving with princely walk to the outbuilding. And then the moon was covered by a cloud and, as if a curtain had come down, it was all darkness.

Michael and Gillian crept back to their beds and fell asleep without a word.

Next morning they were up very early before it was light. They had a hundred miles to travel and they wanted to arrive at their grandparents' house in time for breakfast. Everyone was so busy getting off that the events of the night seemed to Michael and Gillian like a dream that had disappeared with waking.

That Christmas Day seemed very special somehow. Grandma and Grandad were waiting for them all. The old house was decked with holly and winter greenery. The tree looked bigger than ever. The carols in church that morning seemed to go with a great swing and the whole Christmas holiday was a happy celebration.

It was all over too soon and then they were driving back down the road they had come. 'We'll stop for a snack at that inn we found on the way up,' Father said as he drove along.

Gillian and Michael looked at each other and began to remember.

'Good idea,' said Mother.

Within half an hour they were turning off the motorway again and following the road signed to Ayton Rudby. As they approached the village, Mother said, 'We didn't seem to come as far as this on Christmas Eve.'

A few minutes later they had driven right into the centre of the village without seeing any sign of The Star Inn.

'Funny,' said Father. 'We must have driven past without noticing; but it doesn't matter – we can have a snack here.' He parked the car and led the way through the open door of The New Inn.

It was quiet inside and as the snack was being prepared the landlord asked if they were travelling far; a conversation began.

'We stopped at a little inn on the way up,' said Father. 'It was called The Star, but we seemed to pass it without noticing it this morning.'

'You wouldn't notice it,' said the landlord. 'The Star hasn't been hereabouts for seventy years – not since it was pulled down just after Christmas one year – about nineteen ten, that would have been. This inn replaced it; nearer the village, you see. And they called it The New Inn then, and we still call it The New Inn.'

The whole family looked at each other. But the landlord was in full spate and went on, 'They had an old tradition in the village in those days; every Christmas Eve the villagers met at The Star and acted out the Christmas story – seemed appropriate, being The Star and all that. They stopped it after the old inn was closed, but people still talk about it, and there are some who say that on Christmas Eve, if you go to where the old inn stood, you can imagine the old story taking place just as it used to. Just a story, I say,' he finished, and turned to serve another customer.

Driving back they all shared their thoughts about the Christmas holiday.

'Best time we've had for years,' said Mother.

'And none of us quarrelled, or fell out with each other, as we usually do, even though we did start out with bad tempers,' said Father.

'Perhaps it's because we were there,' said Michael.

'Were where?' asked Father.

'Where The Star was,' said Gillian.

'Where what was?' said Father.

'The Star – you know – Christmas Eve and all that,' said Michael.

'We must have been mistaken,' said Mother.

'Unless we went back seventy years,' said Father, and he laughed at the very idea as he eased back into the motorway traffic and headed for home.

Michael and Gillian looked at each other.

'Did we go back seventy years?' whispered Michael.

'Or much further than that?' whispered Gillian back to him.

And they both knew that, wherever they had been, it had been a special Christmas that year.

Roy Chapman

Index of contributors

Index of Key Stages

Key Stage 1

Key Stage 2

Key Stages 1 and 2

Poems

Songs

Stories

Acknowledgements

The publishers gratefully acknowledge permission
to reproduce the following copyright material:

Abingdon Press for 'Thanksgiving' from *Cherry Stones! Garden Swings!' by Ivy O. Eastwick* (1990, Hooper and Woolen); Avon Section Eleven Education Team for 'Manjit goes to the mela' by Sue Punnet and Catherine Short from *The Baisakhi Book* (1987, Avon S. 11 Team); BFSS National RE Centre for 'A Diwali surprise' from *Autumn Term: First Topics*, 'Getting ready for Purim' from *Spring Term: First Topics* and 'Harlequin's new suit' from *Summer Term: First Topics* by Dorothy J. Taylor (1990, BFSS National RE Centre); Behrman House Inc. for 'My Hanukkah Candles' by Philip M. Raskin and 'Rosh Hashanah' by Ben Aronin from *Jolly Jingles for the Jewish Child* (Behrman House Inc.); © 1994 C. J. Bennett for 'The monster and the villagers', 'Nanak reborn', 'Prince Siddhartha is born' and 'The story of Purim'; Berkley Primary School, Heston for 'Guru Nanak' by Class 4B of 1992–1993; © 1994 Ann Bonner for 'Yuan Tan – Chinese New Year'; CAFOD for 'Nduka's Dream' from *At Lowest of Hope* (CAFOD); © 1994 Debbie Campbell for 'Camel caravan song', 'Harvest song' and 'Mrs O'Deary'; CEM for 'An American Indian prayer' by Charles Loloma and 'The ballad of the four sons' from *Exploring a Theme: Harvest* (CEM); The Estate of Leonard Clark for 'Harvest home' by Leonard Clark from *Collected Poems and Verses for Children* (Dobson); © 1994 Narinder Dhami for 'Holi!'; © 1986 Bob Docherty for 'Easter Day' from *Hands Together* (March 1986, Scholastic); EMI for 'Everybody loves Carnival (Saturday) night' by Art Podell (1965, Gregar Music Inc/ EMI Music Inc); Faber & Faber Ltd for 'Easter' by Margaret Joy from *You're in the Juniors now* (1988, Faber & Faber) and 'Seder' by Judith Nicholls from *Dragonsfire* (1990, Faber & Faber); © 1994 John Foster for 'Chinese New Year dragon', 'Holi', 'Janmashtami' and 'Purim'; Garrard Publishing for 'Baking a Hamantash' by Sara G. Levy (1973, Garrard); © 1994 Adèle Geras for 'Different from other nights' (Laura Cecil Literary Agency); Government of India Directorate of Audio and Visual Publicity for 'Vaisakhi is here' from *Indian Express* (April 1993, Indian Express Newspapers Ltd); © 1994 Janet Greenyer for 'The Carnival', 'The First Easter', 'Hannuka', 'The Passover story', 'Purim', 'Raksha Bandhan – Brother's Day' and 'Rosh Hashannah'; © 1994 Grace Hallworth for 'Play mas, Hannah'; © 1994 Theresa Heine for 'A blind girl celebrates Holi', 'Eid-ul-Fitr' and 'A prayer at Ganesha Chaturthi'; Hounslow Language Service for 'Diwali' from *Punjabi Rhymes* by Rajinder Arora and Roz Carter (1990, Hounslow Language Service), 'The Rakhree' and 'This is our Eid' from *Songs of the Sub-Continent* by Keith Lowell (Hounslow Language Service); © 1994 Jean Kenward for 'The birds', 'Festival of fast-breaking', 'Ganesha Chaturthi', 'Guru Nanak's birthday' and 'Wesak'; © 1994 Ian Larmont for 'Egg race' and 'Chinese New Year'; © 1994 Wendy P. Larmont for 'Divali', 'Raksha Bandhan' and 'Wesak'; Lutterworth Press for 'Krishna is born' by Diksha Dalal-Clayton from *The Adventures of Young Krishna* (1991, Lutterworth Press); © 1988 Joan Mellings for 'Christmas in two lands' from *Lion Christmas Book* (1988, Lion Publishing); © 1994 Pratima Mitchell for 'My brother Raja'; © 1994 Tony Mitton for 'Awakening' and 'Divali'; NCEC for 'The Star' by Roy Chapman from *New Stories for Christmas* (1980, NCEC) and 'Village Christmas' by Jean Stolton from *New Stories for Christmas* (1980, NCEC); © 1980 Esther L. Nelson for 'Hanukkah O Hanukkah' from *Holiday Singing and Dancing Games* (1980, Sterling); © 1994 Judith Nicholls for 'Guru Purb – 1', 'Guru Purb – 2', 'Lotus' and 'Sukkot'; Oxford University Press for 'Chinese New Year' by Low Siew Poh and 'The story of Diwali in song' by Punitha Perinparaja from *Festivals* © 1986 Jean Gilbert (1986, OUP); Pavilion Books for 'Holi – Festival of Spring' from *Seasons of Splendour* by Madhur Jaffrey (1985, Pavilion Books); Reed Book Services for 'John and the green dragon' by Jamila Gavin from *The Orange Tree and Other Stories* (1979, Methuen), 'Just enough is plenty' by Barbara Diamond Goldwin (1988, Heinemann) and 'King Poras keeps a promise' by Rani Singh from *The Indian Story Book* (1984, William Heinemann); © 1991 Sujan Rawtani for 'Holi with Shyam' from *Light the Candles* (1991, Cambridge University Press); © 1994 Chris Riley for 'Hanukkah for hope', 'Light the diwa' and 'Shrove Tuesday'; © 1985 Arthur Scholey for 'Elleni and the sharing bread' from *The Johnny Morris Storybook* (1985, BBC); Simon & Schuster Young Books for 'The story of Baisakhi' and 'The wealthy banker of Lahore' from *Stories from the Sikh World* by Rani and Jugnu Singh (1991, Simon & Schuster Young Books); © 1994 Renuka Singh for 'Dakshina and the Queen's necklace', 'Diwali (introduction)', 'Ganesh's broken tusk', 'Indra and Indrana', 'A Krishna story for Raksha Bandhan', 'Radha and Krishna play Holi' and 'Why Ganesh has an elephant's head'; SPI Books for 'Joshua's gelt' by Jacqueline Jacobson Pliskin and 'It's Passover time' by Linda Tsuruoka from *The Jewish Holiday Games and Work Book* (Shapolsky Inc.); © 1991 Dr June Tillman for 'Buddha Lord we offer' from *Light the Candles* (1991, CUP); Tinderbox Music for 'Carnival' by David Moses from *Spring Tinderbox* (1992, A & C Black) © 1992 Tinderbox Music, 'Hanukka candles' by David Moses © 1989 Tinderbox Music, 'Rock a little baby' by David Moses © 1991 Tinderbox Music and 'Symbols of Easter' by David Moses © 1986 Tinderbox Music; The Tribune (Shimla) for 'Festival of Harvest' by Ruchi Chatterji (April 1993, The Tribune Newspaper); Union of American Hebrew Congregations for 'Driedel song' from *Now we begin Driedel song* by Efraim Rosenzweig (UAHC); Walker Books for 'A long time to go' and 'A present for Harvest' from *Will you come on Wednesday?* by Nadya Smith (1987, Walker Books); © 1994 Gill Wilson for 'New life'; Women's League for Conservative Judaism for 'For a good and sweet New Year' by Sadie Rose Weilerstein from *The Singing Way: Poems for Jewish Children* (WLCJ).

Every effort has been made to trace copyright holders for material in this anthology and the publishers apologise for any inadvertant ommissions.